PERSPECTIVES OF THE INDO-PACIFIC REGION: ASPIRATIONS, CHALLENGES AND STRATEGY

PERSPECTIVES OF THE INDO-PACIFIC REGION: ASPIRATIONS, CHALLENGES AND STRATEGY

Edited by

Sandeep Dewan

BASED ON PROCEEDINGS OF
NATIONAL SECURITY SEMINAR 2013
HELD AT USI, NEW DELHI
ON 07-08 NOV 2013

(Established 1870)

United Service Institution of India
New Delhi

Vij Books India Pvt Ltd
New Delhi (India)

Published by

Vij Books India Pvt Ltd
(Publishers, Distributors & Importers)
2/19, Ansari Road
Delhi – 110 002
Phones: 91-11-43596460, 91-11-47340674
Fax: 91-11-47340674
e-mail: vijbooks@rediffmail.com

CONTENTS

CONCEPT NOTE

"Perspectives of the Indo-Pacific Region: Aspirations, Challenges and Strategy"

The end of the Cold War in the nineties saw a decisive shift in power from Europe to Asia. The idea of Asia then broadened to a pan Asia-Pacific community to incorporate the disparate regional architecture under one organisational roof. This debate, off late, has moved on to the term "Indo-Pacific" as it comes at a time when the region is looking to make significant progress to be able to engage in full spectrum of dialogue, cooperation and action on political matters and future challenges related to an all-encompassing wellbeing of the region. Increasing mention of the term 'Indo-Pacific' in strategic discourse today is evidence of the growing prominence of the region as a geo-strategic entity. It signifies the fusion of two geo-politically sensitive and economically vibrant regions, the shores of which are washed by the Indian and the Pacific Oceans. Given the region's vitality, its dynamics is well set to define the future trajectory of political interactions of the 21st century global order.

Historically, maritime and economic activities have been driven by two principal imperatives, the need for resources and markets. The Indo-Pacific Region (IPR), is rich in natural resources, especially hydrocarbons, which fuel the economic engines of the world's economies. The large market gets defined by more than half the world's population inhabiting the IPR. A majority of the world's rising and re-emerging powers such as China, India, South Korea, Australia, Indonesia and Japan are principal constituents of this region. Also the maritime trade flowing through the busy sea lanes of the Indo-Pacific region is vital not only for the economic prosperity of the region but beyond as well.

The IPR's economic strength, military power, and political

dynamism will make it the world's most important region in the coming decades, and its significance will be felt throughout the globe. The IPR includes the waters, islands, and littoral states stretching from the mid-Pacific to the seas West of the Indian subcontinent. It includes a population of nearly 4 billion people, three of the world's largest economies, seven of the ten smallest nations, the world's largest democracy, the world's smallest republic, nine of the world's ten largest ports, seven of the ten largest standing militaries, five of the world's declared nuclear armed nations and a combined GDP of nearly $ 20 trillion at PPP terms. Since the end of World War II, the region has transformed itself into the world's economic powerhouse, yet it remains driven by distrust, territorial disputes, ethnic tensions and painful memories.

The IPR faces a full spectrum of threats from low intensity of conflict to a nuclearised neighbourhood. It is located at the focus of an arc of fundamentalist activism, terrorism and political instability. There are unresolved territorial and boundary issues within states. The IPR is hemmed by an unfavorable nuclear and missile environment and proliferation of weapons of mass destruction. Coupled with this is the fact that instability of failing states in the IPR provides a very fertile breeding ground for terrorists and fundamentalism. Maritime security is another source of concern considering the region's maritime dependence. The Tunisian sparked Jasmine Revolution flamed by the social media has become a movement of sorts in many states of the IPR. The movement has grown in intensity due to problems of unemployment, inflation, corruption, lack of freedom of speech and poor living conditions, issues which are endemic to the IPR.

The IPR has already been a scene of multiple wars between large and small powers. Unresolved territorial disputes remain a destabilising factor across the region and a number of them could spark future conflicts and skirmishes. Also massive military build-up by some regional powers and assertive behaviour coupled with willingness to use force, should be a cause for global concern. Sea Lines of Communication or SLOCs are an instrument of maritime power with geography being the determining factor for forces being deployed to support friends or deter enemies. Any unexplained or unwarranted military buildup or acquisition of forces can lead to military imbalance and mutual distrust. Any undue assertiveness or willingness to use force to support unilaterally declared claims could become a potential trigger for a skirmish at sea, with grave consequences.

The US military presence is not new to the region. The US has historic defence treaties with its regional allies, Australia, Japan, Philippines, South Korea and Thailand and a policy of strategic ambiguity towards Taiwan. The new policy of "US Pivot to the Asia-Pacific" announced in January 2012 was motivated by the need to respond to the growing assertiveness of some regional powers as also to reassure its regional allies. So the pieces have been set for this grand game of chess and some moves already made. But how this very complicated, multi-actor, multi-scenario game will eventually play out is anyone's guess.

The IPR has, off late, become the new frontline of the current manifestation of cyber warfare with various types of cyber weapons being deployed by parties whose identities can only be speculated upon, but presumed to be state and non-state actors from within the region and beyond. Cyber-attacks can have devastating results in terms of loss of livelihood, destruction of the economy and anarchy in society. Loss of life alone can no longer be a barometer of devastation. It is as important to have contingency plans ready to deal with all eventualities, as it is for countries to come together to nip this scourge in the bud, and to call out the rogue actors.

In the sub-conventional arena, terrorist groups have established deep roots in the IPR, and are operating across national boundaries with increasing impunity. Piracy and its nexus with maritime terrorism, illegal trade in arms, drug smuggling and human trafficking, are generating significant instability in several countries. Additionally, there are several other lower end threats that require constabulary responses.

The IPR today confronts a great resource dilemma at a time of fast-growing demand for water, hydrocarbons, minerals, and other natural resources. This crunch has given rise to a new Great Game centered on rival plans to secure a larger share of strategic resources. The way oil shaped international geopolitics in the twentieth century;

the competition over water resources is set to shape many interstate relationships in this century. The exercise of hydro leverage can prompt a downstream state to build up its military capabilities to help counterbalance the riparian disadvantage.

The IPR is also frequented by natural disasters, with about 70 percent of the occurrences worldwide confined to this region alone. High population density and lack of capacity in the littoral, only accentuate the resultant human suffering. On the global warming front, if current estimates on the Arctic meltdown come true, we in the Indo-Pacific could be staring at humanitarian and environmental crises of debilitating proportions.

Given the world's focus on the Indo-Pacific, it would be in order to take a de-novo look at the changing geopolitics and its effects on the region and on its stakeholders and their strategic priorities. There is an increasing desire within the region towards tackling common challenges and creating politico-security architecture to promote growth and prosperity, peace and stability. It is about focusing the aspirations and the destinies of the people of this region on a common path. With globalisation and the consequent compression of geographic spaces, 'Indo-Pacific' has come to reflect contemporary realities.

History has shown that rising powers inevitably trample upon their rivals' natural spheres of influence. We, in the Indo-Pacific, need to work towards a security construct that leverages the civilisational linkages to expand cooperation and build partnership across the Indo-Pacific. Broadly, therefore, the Seminar on "Perspectives on Indo-Pacific Region: Aspirations, Challenges and Strategy" is built around themes of national aspirations, regional security challenges and generation of strategic options. Efforts need to be devoted to making recommendations for a better and brighter future for the Indo-Pacific Region and for the rest of the international community.

PARTICIPANTS

Lieutenant General PK Singh, PVSM, AVSM (Retd)

Lieutenant General PK Singh, was commissioned as a 2/Lt in the Indian Army in 1967. He retired as an Army Commander (C-in-C) in 2008. He is a graduate of Higher Command Course and the National Defence College. His academic qualifications include MSc, MPhil and Post-graduate Diploma in Business Management.

He took over as Director of the United Service Institution of India in January 2009. He is a member of the IISS, London and a Council Member of the Indian Council of World Affairs, New Delhi. He is an Adviser to the Fair Observer, USA.

His articles have been published in "The NIDS Journal", Tokyo; in "Global Security – The Growing Challenges", USA. He has also written for the book, "The China-India Nuclear Crossroads" edited by Lora Salman. He has written a chapter for the forthcoming "Oxford handbook on UN Peacekeeping Operations". He has edited the book "Comprehensive National Power – A Model for India" and the book "Civilian Capacity Building for Peace Operations".

Lieutenant General Ajay Kumar Singh, PVSM, AVSM, SM, VSM (Retd)

Lieutenant General AK Singh, PVSM, AVSM, SM, VSM, (Retd) is the Lieutenant Governor of the Andaman and Nicobar Islands. He was a former, General Officer, Commanding-in-Chief, Southern Command. An alumnus of National Defence Academy, he was commissioned into the 7th Light Cavalry on the 17 June 1973. Known for his high integrity and professionalism, the General is looked upon as a role model by large numbers in the Armed Forces.

He attended the Staff College at Camberley in the United Kingdom, having topped the staff college entrance examination; Malinovski Tank Academy in Moscow; Royal College of Military

Science, United Kingdom and the renowned National Defence Colleges in India and in Sweden. He achieved top honours in every course that he attended both in India and abroad, achieving the unique distinction of being the only officer to be trained both in Russia and NATO, at the height of the Cold War. He has an MSc and MPhil in Defence Studies in addition to his military qualifications.

He headed the foreign division of the Indian Army, dealing with Defence Cooperation with many foreign countries. He has held the challenging assignment of Director General, Perspective Planning, where he was responsible for all strategies, development of long-term perspectives and transformation of the Indian Army into the 21st century, including long term budgeting. He has represented the country and the Armed Forces in many high powered delegations to major countries. He is credited with profound understanding of Strategic and National level issues and concerns, and is a regular speaker at the National Defence College and other important institutions.

Ambassador Lalit Mansingh, Former Foreign Secretary

Ambassador Lalit Mansingh served as the foreign secretary of India from 1999 to 2001 and the Indian Ambassador to the United States from 2001 to 2004. He was also the High Commissioner to the United Kingdom. His other assignments include High Commissioner to Nigeria (1993-95) and Ambassador to the United Arab Emirates (1980-83). Ambassador Mansingh was also the Dean of the Foreign Service Institute of India and the Director-General for the Indian Council of Cultural Relations.

Ambassador Gleb A Ivashentsov

Ambassador Gleb A Ivashentsov graduated from International Economic Relations Faculty, Moscow State Institute of International Relations, USSR Ministry of Foreign Affairs. He was in the USSR Ministry of Foreign Trade from 1967-1969. He was thereafter with the International Department, Central Committee, and Communist Party of the Soviet Union from 1969-1975. Further from 1991-1995, he was a Consul General of USSR / Russia in Bombay, India. He was also the Ambassador of Russia to the Union of Myanmar and the Republic of Korea. From 2001-2005, he was the Director,

Third, Second Asian Department (South and Southwest Asia), Russia Ministry of Foreign Affairs.

During his tenure as Ambassador to the Republic of Korea he made personal contribution to the advancement of Russian-South Korean cooperation in energy, including peaceful use of nuclear energy, and space exploration. He was awarded the Order of Friendship (Russia) in 2003 and Khanhwa Medal for diplomatic merits (Republic of Korea) in 2009. He has to his credit a number of books on international relations published in Russia, India and the Republic of Korea. His recent publications are: "India – basics in brief" in Russian (2009) and "Behind the fortifications of 38th parallel. Reflections of the Ambassador of Russia to South Korea" in Russian and Korean (2012). His Diplomatic rank is Ambassador Extraordinary and Plenipotentiary. He is a Special Research Fellow of the China Center for Contemporary World Studies.

Major General BK Sharma, AVSM, SM** (Retd)

Major General BK Sharma was commissioned in infantry in 1976 and commanded 6 SIKHLI. He is pursuing his PhD in Geopolitics in Central Asia. He is a graduate of Staff College, Higher Command and National Defence College. He has tenanted prestigious command, instructional and staff appointments, notably, Senior Faculty Member at National Defence College, New Delhi, Command of a Mountain Division and Brigadier General Staff (both assignments on China Border) Principal Director Net Assessment at HQ Integrated Defence Staff, Defence Attaché in Embassy of India in Kazakhstan and Kyrgyzstan, and UN Military Observer in Central America.

He regularly contributes articles to prestigious journals in India and abroad. He regularly participates in international seminars in India and abroad. Presently, he is working as Distinguished Fellow at the United Service Institution of India, New Delhi. He specializes in Net Assessment, Scenario Building and Strategic Gaming. He conducts strategic games for the National Defence College and Higher Command Courses of the Army, Navy and Air force.

Mr. Tetsuo Kotani

Mr Tetsuo Kotani is a Special Research Fellow, at Okazaki Institute,

Tokyo and a Senior Research Fellow at the Research Institute for Peace and Security (RIPS), Tokyo. He is a member of the International Advisory Board, at Project 2049 Institute in Washington, and a nonresident SPF fellow at Pacific Forum CSIS in Honolulu. He was a research fellow at Ocean Policy Research Foundation (OPRF) from 2006-2010. His dissertation is on the strategic implications of home porting US carriers in Japan. His other research interests include US-Japan relations, international relations and maritime security in the Asia-Pacific region. He was a visiting fellow at the US-Japan Center at Vanderbilt University. He received a security studies fellowship from the Research Institute for Peace and Security (RIPS). He won the 2003 Japanese Defence Minister Prize.

Dr Victor V Sumsky

Dr Victor Sumsky is currently the Director, ASEAN Centre in MGIMO-University (Moscow State Institute for International Relations, Russian Ministry of Foreign Affairs) and Chief Research Fellow, Institute of World Economy and International Relations, Russian Academy of Sciences. He was also a Senior Research Fellow, Head of Section of Institute of World Economy and International Relations, USSR/Russian Academy of Sciences. He has a Doctorate of Sciences (History) from the Institute of World Economy and International Relations, Russian Academy of Sciences and a doctorate from the Institute of Oriental Studies, USSR Academy of Sciences. His areas of interest are Political development of Southeast Asian nations, ASEAN, Asian regionalism and Security, and international relations in East Asia.

He is member of the Russian National Committee and Council for Security Cooperation in the Asia Pacific, along with being a member of the Board, European Association of Southeast Asian Studies. He is also a Visiting Professor at The Henry M Jackson School of International Studies, University of Washington, Seattle, Visiting Fellow at the Center for International Studies, London School of Economics and Political Science and Center for Integrative and Development Studies, University of the Philippines.

Some of his publications are "ASEAN-Russia: Foundations and Future Prospects", "Russia as a Euro pacific Power", "New Trends in

Asian Regional Architecture and Russia's Role", "Russia in the Asia-Pacific Region: Problems of Security and Cooperation", "Changing Security Dynamics in Southeast Asia and 21st Century" and "China: Globalization of Security Interests". He has also written articles in Soviet/ Russian academic journals (including World Economy and International Relations, International Affairs, Asia and Africa Today, Security Index), Alternatives (New York), Philippine Studies (Quezon City), The Japanese Journal of American Studies (Tokyo), Global Asia (Seoul).

Professor Edward I-Hsin Chen

Prof Edward I-Hsin Chen did his PhD from Department of Political Science, Columbia University. He is currently teaching at the Graduate Institute of Americas (GIA), at Tamkang University, Taiwan, Republic of China. He was a legislator from 1996 to 1999, a national assemblyman in 2005, and director of the institute from 2001 to 2005.

He specializes in US governance, international relations theories, globalisation and international political economy, decision-making theories of US policy toward China and Taiwan and US-China-Taiwan relations. His recent articles include "The Implications of Taiwan Strait Peace As One of US-Japan Common Strategic Objectives for Cross-Strait Relations and the Security of Taiwan".

Vice Admiral Arun Kumar Singh, PVSM, AVSM, NM (Retd)

Vice Admiral Arun Kumar Singh retired in 2007, after 40 years service in the Indian Navy. During his service career he commanded various warships, submarines, submarine squadrons and a submarine base. He has sailed extensively in the Indian, Atlantic and Pacific Oceans in submarines and warships, and has exercised with various Navies and Coast Guards of South East Asia and Asia Pacific Region. In early 1971, as navigating officer of a frigate he operated off Sri Lanka (as part of an Indian Navy task force) when that nation was facing a threat from the JVP. In 1989 he served with the Indian Peace Keeping Force (IPKF) in Sri Lanka as Indian Navy Commander, Trincomalee. In mid December 2004, as DG Indian Coast Guard, he visited Sri Lanka for the first ever Indian Coast Guard (ICG) – Sri Lankan Navy (SLN) joint exercise.

A specialist in navigation & fighter direction, submarines and missiles, he completed specialist courses at the Frunze Academy (St Petersburg, Russia) and the Admiral Makharov Academy (Vladivostok, Russia). He is an alumnus of the National Defence College (India), Naval War College (India), Defence Services Staff College (India), and holds MSc degree (defence and strategic studies) from Madras University and separate certificates of service, 'Master Foreign Going Ships' from the Governments of India and United Kingdom.

Vice Admiral AK Singh has held the posts of Director of Tactics, Director Submarine Operations, Flag Officer Submarines, Assistant Chief of Naval Staff (Submarines) and Controller of Personnel Services at Naval Headquarters; Flag Officer Commanding Eastern Fleet at Vishakapatnam and the Director General of the Indian Coast Guard at Coast Guard Headquarters, New Delhi. He was the Commander-in-Chief of the Joint Andaman and Nicobar Command, at Port Blair and Commander-in-Chief, Eastern Naval Command at Vishakhapatnam before retirement.

Post retirement, Vice Admiral Arun Kumar Singh is a Council Member of the USI, New Delhi, and a participant in India-Pakistan Track 2 discussions. He has addressed various military institutions, universities, think tanks and symposiums in India and abroad.

Rear Admiral Sumihiko Kawamura (Retd)

Rear Admiral Sumihiko Kawamura (Retd) joined the Japan Maritime Self Defence Force (JMSDF) in 1960, after graduating from the National Defence Academy. A graduate of JMSDF Staff College and the National Institute for Defence Studies, the maritime patrol aircraft pilot has held a number of prestigious staff and command appointments. This includes tenures as Naval Attaché in Washington DC, and Vice President, Joint Staff College, and Commanders of Fleet Air Wing Five and Four at Naha, Okinawa and at Atsugi, respectively. In 1998, he established the Kawamura Institute for maritime strategic studies in Abiko, Japan. He is the Vice President of the Okazaki Institute and Representative the Kawamura Institute. He has been an active contributor of regional dialogues on maritime and security issues and has participated in many international conferences. He retired from JMSDF in 1991.

Lieutenant General Wallace "Chip" Gregson, Jr (Retd)

Lieutenant General Wallace "Chip" Gregson is the Senior Director of China and the Pacific. Lt Gen Gregson is a retired Marine Lieutenant General and was Assistant Secretary of Defence for Asian and Pacific Security Affairs in 2009 and held the post until April 2011. Previously, he served as Commander, US Marine Corps Forces Pacific; Commanding General, Fleet Marine Force, Pacific; and Commander, US Marine Corps Bases, Pacific. After his retirement in 2005, he joined the US Olympic Committee and formed his own consulting company.

Rear Admiral Sudarshan Shrikhande

Rear Admiral Sudarshan Shrikhande is a graduate of the National Defence Academy and was commissioned on 01 Jul 1980. His early sea tenures were on IN Ships Taragiri, LCU-L32 and Rajput. From 1985 to 1988 he underwent the ASW Weapon and Sonar Engineering Course at the Soviet Naval War College, Leningrad (St Petersburg). He graduated with distinction in MSc in Weapon and Sonar Engineering. He served as ASWO/Ops officer of INS Ranvir for nearly four years. Further he was in Command of INS Nishank and INS Kora and Executive Officer of INS Delhi. His ashore appointments included Instructor ASW School, Commander War Room at NHQ, Director Indian Navy Tactical Evaluation Group and Directing Staff at College of Naval Warfare. He was the Defence Adviser in Canberra, Australia concurrently accredited to Fiji, New Zealand, Papua New Guinea and Tonga from 2005-2008. He commanded INS Rajput in the Eastern Fleet from Apr 2008 – May 2009. On promotion to Flag Rank, he was ACNS (Foreign Co-operation Intelligence) at NHQ till Aug 2010. His previous appointment was as Chief of Staff, SNC from Aug 2010 - Aug 2012.

He is a graduate of the Defence Services Staff College in 1995 and was awarded the Scudder Medal. He has completed the Naval Higher Command Course at the College of Naval Warfare, Mumbai. He is also a 2003 graduate of the US Naval War College, Newport, Rhode Island, where he graduated with highest distinction and was awarded the "Robert Bateman" and Jerome E Levy" Prizes and the "James Forrestal" Seminar Prize.

Rear Admiral K Raja Menon (Retd)

Admiral Menon retired in 1994 as the Assistant Chief of Naval Staff (Operations). He headed the group that wrote the Indian Navy's New Maritime Strategy. He recently retired as the Chairman of the Task Force on Net Assessment and Simulation in the National Security Council. He is a distinguished fellow in the Institute of Peace and Conflict Studies and the National Maritime Foundation.

His published work includes, 'Maritime Strategy and Continental Wars', 'A Nuclear Strategy for India' and 'The Indian Navy: A Photo Essay'. He has also edited books like 'Weapons of Mass Destruction: Options for India'; An Occasional Paper: 'The US-India Non-proliferation Divide: the Way Ahead' by Cooperative Monitoring Center, Sandia in 2005 and 'The Long View from Delhi: The Grand Strategy of Indian Foreign Policy' published in India and the US, 2010.

His areas of expertise are Nuclear Strategy, Maritime Strategy, Net Assessment and Strategic Scenarios, both Politico-Military and Technological and Politico-Military Simulation and Gaming.

Dr Tzong-Ho Bau

Dr Tzong-Ho Bau is the Vice-Chairman of the Prospect Foundation; Professor, Department of Political Science, National Taiwan University. He graduated from NTU, Department of Political Science, in 1974 and received a doctorate degree from University of Texas at Austin in 1986.

He established the Institute for Advanced Studies in Humanities and Social Sciences in 2005 and served as the founding Dean from October 2005 to March 2008. In collaboration with European Commission and the NTU, Dr Bau established the European Union Centre in Taiwan in 2009 and was appointed as the founding Director General of the Centre till March 2011. He is now the President of the ROC Association of International Relations. He was the President of Chinese Association of Political Science (Taipei) from 1993 to 1995.

He was the trustee of the Foundation on Asia-Pacific Peace Studies from 2008 to 2009.

Dr Bau's expertise is in the field of international relations theory, foreign policy decision-making, international conflicts, US foreign policy, US diplomatic history, game theory and Cross-strait relations.

Colonel (Dr) Thomas X Hammes (Retd)

In his thirty years in the US Marine Corps, TX Hammes served at all levels, including command of a rifle company, a weapons company, an intelligence battalion, an infantry battalion and the Chemical Biological Incident Response Force. He served as battalion fire support coordinator, regimental S-2 and S-4, Division G-2, G-3 Plans, G-3 Operations and G-3 Training. He also served as MEF and Fleet Plans Officer. He participated in stabilization operations in Somalia and Iraq.

Hammes has a Masters in Historical Research and a Doctorate in Modern History, from Oxford University. He is currently a Distinguished Research Fellow at the Institute for National Strategic Studies, National Defence University. He is also an Adjunct Professor at Georgetown University.

He is the author of "The Sling and the Stone: On War in the Twenty-First Century" and "Forgotten Warriors: The 1st Provisional Marine Brigade, the Corps Ethos, and the Korean War". He has written chapters in nearly 13 books, over 100 articles and opinion pieces have been published in newspapers, academic and professional journals like Washington Post, New York Times, and Jane's Defence Weekly. He has lectured widely at US and International Staff and War Colleges.

Professor Cai Penghong

Prof Cai Penghong is a Senior Fellow at the Shanghai Institute for International Studies (SIIS). He graduated from Fudan University in 1982, with a degree in International Politics. His research and teaching expertise are in the field of international relations and security in East Asia, with special emphasis on China's foreign policy and maritime security and strategy in Asia. He is also a member of Maritime Study Center, Foundation of China's International Studies in Beijing. In

1992-1993 he became a fellow at the East-West Center, Hawaii. In 1995 he was a visiting scholar at Graduate School of Pacific Studies and International Relations, University of California, San Diego.

Shri Mohan Guruswamy

Mohan Guruswamy had his undergraduate education in Mathematics, Physics and Chemistry at Nizam College, Hyderabad, India. He has post-graduate qualifications in Public Policy, International Affairs and Management. He is an alumnus of the John F Kennedy School of Government, Harvard University and the Graduate School of Business, Stanford University. He is the author of several books on policy issues, some of the recent being The Looming Crisis in India's Agriculture; India: Issues in Development; India's World: Essays in Foreign Policy and Security Issues; India China Relations: The Border Issue and Beyond; and the latest being Chasing the Dragon: Will India Catch-up with China? He is a frequent commentator on national and international print and electronic media on matters of current interest. His papers on Redefining Poverty, Income Inequality, Backwardness of Bihar, Economic Development in West Bengal, and FDI in Retail have been published in well-regarded journals like the Economic and Political Weekly, Seminar and the Journal of Public Policy, UK.

Mohan Guruswamy regularly lectures at institutions such as the Observer Research Foundation, Indian Institute of Public Administration, Army War College, Colleges of Air and Naval Warfare, and the National Defence College, trade and industry associations, and educational institutions in India and abroad. Mohan Guruswamy has also been invited to speak on economic and security policy issues at the Centre for International Development, Harvard University; the Heritage Foundation, Atlantic Council, and German Marshall Fund US; Russiky Mir Foundation, Moscow; Futuribles International, Paris: Institute for Economics at the China Academy for Social Sciences: China Economics Society, China Institute for Contemporary International Relations and the China Reform Forum. He is also a Distinguished Fellow of the Institute of Peace and Conflict Studies, New Delhi; Non-resident Senior Fellow of the Atlantic Council, Washington DC and serves on the Board of Management of the United Service Institution of India, New Delhi.

Mr U Kyee Myint

U Kyee Myint graduated from the Yangoon University in 1969 and joined the Myanmar Foreign Service in 1972. He served in various capacities in the Departments of the Ministry of Foreign Affairs, as well as in the Myanmar Missions abroad, including Myanmar Missions in East Berlin, Bern, Geneva, Bonn, Dhaka and London, where he attended many International Conferences and Meetings. He retired from the Foreign Service in December 2006 as Deputy Director-General of the ASEAN Department of the Ministry of Foreign Affairs. From January 2007 to December 2007, he worked as Secretary, of the Myanmar Institute of the Strategic and International Studies, at the Ministry of Foreign Affairs.

He was appointed again as a Member of the Myanmar Institute of Strategic and International Studies when it was reorganized as an independent Institute attached to the Ministry of Foreign Affairs in January 2013.

Lieutenant Colonel Nguyen The Hong

Lt Col Nguyen The Hong got enlisted in the Army in 1990. He was a cadet in military college from 1991 to 1995. He did training courses in Military College of Foreign Languages, 1991-1995; Academy of Military Science, 2001-2003; China's Peking University, 2006-2007; and China's University for Political Science and Law, 2009-2012.

He was a Research Assistant in Institute for Defence Strategic Studies from 1995 to 2000 and a Research Assistant in IDIR from 2001 to 2005. He was Deputy Defence Attaché of Vietnam to China from 2009 to 2012. Currently he is Head of Asia-Africa Division of IDIR. His expertise is on defence and security issues in Asia – Pacific region, especially on China.

Ambassador Leela K Ponappa, IFS (Retd)

Ambassador Leela K Ponappa was the Deputy National Security Advisor and Secretary, National Security Council Secretariat from May 2007 till October 2009. Ambassador Ponappa was a career diplomat and joined the Indian Foreign Service in 1970. Her last appointment was as Ambassador to the Netherlands and Permanent

Representative to the Organisation for the Prohibition of Chemical Weapons. She was also Ambssador to Thailand and Permanent Representative of India to UNESCAP (2002-2004).

Earlier, at the Ministry of External Affairs in New Delhi, Ambassador Ponappa held several positions including Additional Secretary for Bangladesh, Sri Lanka, Myanmar and Maldives (1998-2001), Joint Secretary in charge of the Consular, Passport, Visa and Overseas Indians Division (1992-1994) and for the South Asian Association for Regional Cooperation (SAARC).

She was seconded to the faculty of the National Defence College, New Delhi, from 1995-1998 as Senior Directing Staff. She was Research Associate at the Centre for South and Southeast Asia, University of California, Berkeley. She also dealt with India's relations with Pakistan and Afghanistan from 1975-78 at the Ministry of External Affairs (MEA). She has also dealt with India's relations with its neighbours, covering a wide range of issues which included border negotiations; national security issues including terrorism and narcotics; sharing of river waters, disaster management and infrastructure projects; economic affairs including India-US trade and investment, negotiation and implementation of the India-Sri Lanka Free Trade Agreement; regional cooperation through SAARC, BIMSTEC and UNESCAP.

Brigadier General (Dr) Chol-Ho Chong (Retd)

Dr Chol-Ho Chong has worked as a research fellow in the Department of Security at the Sejong Institute, since 2009. He was a fighter pilot, who received his BA from the Korea Air Force Academy in 1972. During his 31 years of service he has commanded a number of units from squadron to wing-level in the Republic of Korea Air Force (RoKAF). He was promoted to Brigadier General in 1996, and he participated in United Nations Command, Military Armistice Commission (UNC/MAC) as a delegate of the RoK in 2000. He served as the Commander of the Air University, RoKAF from 2001 to 2002. After his retirement in July 2002, General Chong worked as a consultant to the Director-General, the Organization for the Prohibition of Chemical Weapons (OPCW), The Hague, Netherlands.

In 2008 he received his PhD in international relations from the Graduate School of International Studies, the Korea University. He has written articles concerning UNC, OPCON transfer, NPT regime and North Korea security and arms control issues. Currently he is a visiting Professor at SookMyung Women's University in Seoul, teaching college students; 'International Security Strategy'. His research areas include International Conflicts and Security Strategy, WMD Nonproliferation Regime and Nuclear Strategy, Security Relations in Northeast Asia, NATO Strategy, RoK, US Military Strategy, RoK-US Alliance and UNC.

General Chong has been awarded military Chonsu medal and Presidential Citations from the RoK Government, an Air Commendation medal from the USAF, and Legion of Merit from US government during his military service.

Vice Admiral Pradeep Kaushiva, UYSM, VSM (Retd)

Vice Admiral Kaushiva commanded Indian Naval Ships Prachand and Veer, Coast Guard Ship Vijaya and the Guided Missile Frigate INS Ganga. He was the Fleet Communications and Electronic Warfare Officer, Western Fleet and Fleet Operations Officer, Eastern Fleet. He was Director Naval Signals and Electronic Warfare and Director Naval Operations at Naval Headquarters. After promotion to the Flag Rank, he was Assistant Chief of Naval Staff (Information Warfare and Operations); Deputy Commandant and Chief Instructor, National Defence Academy at Khadakwasla; Flag Officer Commanding Eastern Fleet and Chief of Staff, Southern Naval Command at Kochi. As Vice Admiral, he was the Commandant of the Naval Academy at Ezhimala, Kerala. He takes keen interest in strategic maritime affairs and has been participating in seminars, discussions and dialogues on related matters in India and abroad.

He was decorated by the President with Vishist Seva Medal in 1993 and Uttam Yudh Seva Medal in 1997 for distinguished service of exceptional order.

Major General (Dr) Nguyen Hong Quan

Dr Nguyen Hong Quan is currently the Vice Director General of the Vietnam Institute for Defence Strategy (IDS). His primary research interest is Southeast Asia military and security. He is the author of over 60 articles in academic journals. Before joining the IDS, he was Vice Director General of Foreign Relations Department.

He graduated from the Institut International d'Administration Public in Paris, France and from the Vietnam National Defence Academy. He also received his Master of Arts in International Relations from the Diplomatic Academy of Vietnam and a Doctorate in World History from the Vietnam National University, Hanoi.

He attended the Republic of France Institut de Hautes Etudes de Defence Nationale and is a Lecturer at Vietnam National Defence Academy.

Professor (Ms) Ruhanas Harun

Ruhanas Harun is professor and Director of Centre for Defence and International Security Studies at National Defence University, Malaysia. Prior to this she was Head of Strategic Studies Departments, National University of Malaysia and the University of Malaya. She has lectured and published research papers on foreign policy, national security and international politics.

Ruhanas Harun obtained her BA (Hons) in International Relations from the University of Malaya, Kuala Lumpur, did her MA in International Relations from the University of Sorbonne, Paris, and Post Graduate Diploma in Political studies from the Institute of Political Studies, France. She has taught extensively in Malaysia and abroad, including at the Malaysian Armed Forces Staff College, Armed Forces Defence College, the University of Cairo, Egypt, Universitas Pembangunan Nasional, and Jogjakarta. She is frequently consulted by government agencies and the media on international affairs.

Apart from being an expert on Malaysia's national security, Ruhanas Harun is also an illustrious expert on Indochina and Malaysia's foreign relations. She has contributed widely in academic fields and written articles in newspapers also. Current research interests include nation-building in Malaysia and regionalism and politics in Middle East.

Smt Sujatha Singh, Foreign Secretary

Smt Sujatha Singh was born in July 1954 and joined the Indian Foreign Service in July 1976. She assumed charge as Foreign Secretary on 01 August 2013.

Prior to taking over as Foreign Secretary, Smt Singh served as Ambassador of India to Germany (2012-2013) and High Commissioner to Australia (2007-2012).

She started her overseas assignments as Second Secretary in the Embassy of India, Bonn (1978-82). Subsequently she was First Secretary, High Commission of India, Accra (1985-89), Counselor, Embassy of India, Paris (1989-92), Deputy Chief of Mission and Deputy Permanent Representative to ESCAP at Embassy of India, Bangkok (1997-2000) and Consul General, Milan (2000-04).

Smt Singh has served over a third of her career at Headquarters. She was Under Secretary looking after Nepal (1982-85), Director, Economic Co-ordination Unit (1992-95), attended the National Defence College at New Delhi (1995) and Joint Secretary at the Foreign Service Institute, New Delhi (1996-97). Subsequently she was Joint Secretary and then Additional Secretary responsible for West Europe and the EU in the Ministry of External Affairs, New Delhi (2004-07).

Other Participants

1. Vice Adm Hideaki Kaneda (Retd), Japan.

2. Lt Gen Takayoshi Ogawa (Retd), Japan.

3. Dr Wen – Hsien Vincent Chen, Taiwan.

4. Mr Yang-Ming Sun, Taiwan.

5. Mr Yu-Hsun Chang, Taiwan.

6. Dr James E Auer, USA.

7. Col Grant F Newsham, USA.

8. Maj Vu Cao Dinh, Vietnam.

9. Capt Duong Bui Trung, Vietnam.

ACRONYMS

Short Form	Full Form
A2AD	Anti-Access and Area-Denial
ACNS	Assistant Chief of Naval Staff
ADSOM	ASEAN Defense Senior Officials Meeting
APEC	Asia Pacific Economic Cooperation
APR	Asia Pacific Region
ARF	ASEAN Regional Forum
ASB	Air-Sea Battle
ASEAN	Association of South East Asian Nations
ASWO	Anti-Submarine Warfare Officer
BIMSTEC	Bay of Bengal Initiative for Multi-Sectoral Technical and Economic Cooperation
BRICS	Brazil Russia India China South Africa
CEPEA	Comprehensive Economic Partnership in East Asia
CNP	Comprehensive National Power
COC	Code of Conduct in the South China Sea
CONUS	Continental United States
CSAF	Chief of Staff United States Air Force
CSBA	Centre for Strategic and Budgetary Assessments.
DOC	Declaration on the Conduct of Parties in the South China Sea
EAFTA	East Asia Free Trade Agreement
EAS	East Asia Summit

ECFA	Economic Cooperation Framework Agreement
ECS	East China Sea
EEZ	Exclusive Economic Zone
ESCAP	Economic and Social Commission for Asia and Pacific
EU	European Union
FDI	Foreign Direct Investment
FTA	Free Trade Agreement
FTAAP	Free Trade Area of the Asia-Pacific
ICAO	International Civil Aviation Organisation
IDS	Institute for Defense Strategy
IFS	Indian Foreign Service
IPR	Indo-Pacific Region
ISR	Intelligence Surveillance and Reconnaissance
LCS	Littoral Combat Ship
LCU	Landing Craft Utility
MEA	Ministry of External Affairs
MMCA	Military Maritime Consultative Agreement
MOOTW	Military Operations Other Than War
NATO	North Atlantic Treaty Organisation
NDA	National Defence Academy
NHQ	Naval Headquarters
NIDS	National Institute of Defense Strategy
NSR	Northern Sea Routes
NTU	National Taiwan University
NWFP	North West Frontier Province
OECD	Organisation for Economic Cooperation and

	Development
OPCW	Organisation for Prohibition of Chemical Weapons
PLA	People's Liberation Army
PLAAF	People's Liberation Army Air Force
PLAN	People's Liberation Army Navy
PRC	People's Republic of China
RCEP	Regional Comprehensive Economic Partnership
RIC	Russia India China
RIMPAC	Rim of the Pacific Exercise
ROC	Republic of China
SAARC	South Asian Association for Regional Cooperation
SCO	Shanghai Co-operation Organisation
SCS	South China Sea
SLBM	Submarine Launched Ballistic Missile
SLOCs	Sea Lines of Communications
SSBN	Ballistic Missile Nuclear Powered Submarine
TIFA	Trade and Investment Framework Agreement
TPP	Trans Pacific Partnership
UAV	Unmanned Aerial Vehicle
UNC/MAC	United Nations Command Military Armistice Commission
UNESCAP	United Nations Economic and Social Commission for Asia and the Pacific
USAF	United States Air Force
USSR	The Union of Soviet Socialist Republics
V/STOL	Vertical/Short Take off and Landing

INAUGURAL SESSION

Welcome Address - Lieutenant General PK Singh,
PVSM, AVSM (Retd) Director USI.

Inaugural Address - Lt Gen Ajay Kumar Singh, PVSM,
AVSM, SM,VSM (Retd),
Lt Governor Andaman and Nicobar Islands.

WELCOME ADDRESS

Lieutenant General PK Singh, PVSM, AVSM (Retd) Director, USI

General AK Singh, Air Chief Marshal SP Tyagi, Members of the USI Council, Excellencies, distinguished participants of the conference, ladies and gentlemen.

It is my privilege to welcome you to the international seminar that we have every year in November focusing on the Indo-Pacific region. To many of you who have been attending the seminars, you will recall that this is fifth consecutive year that we are hosting this seminar. There was a request from our previous participants that we need to have linkages between the Indian Ocean and Western Pacific and also that India's role in both the areas needs to be understood.

I would like to thank our 22 foreign participants who have taken the trouble to be here with us. We are honoured by your presence and I hope you are being looked after well by the USI staff. We have benefited by your presence. I would like to say that we are extremely honoured to have General AK Singh, PVSM, AVSM, SM, VSM, Lieutenant Governor of Andaman and Nicobar Islands, who will deliver the inaugural address.

We have absolutely frank and open discussions since USI is an academic institution. We do not hold anything back and please feel free to interact. I would request all the participants and the panelists to convey their views and concerns to us openly and frankly. Once again thank you for being here.

I would also like to thank the Ministry of External Affairs (MEA) for supporting us in our endeavours since the last five years.

INAUGURAL ADDRESS

Lieutenant General Ajay Kumar Singh, PVSM, AVSM, SM,VSM (Retd)
Lieutenant Governor Andaman and Nicobar Islands

Introduction

At the very outset let me commend the effort of USI in organizing this annual event on the Indo-Pacific Region – I thank them for inviting me to deliver the Inaugural Address.

Let me confess that till very recently while in uniform, I was more concerned and focused on our land borders, though I was conscious of our increasing maritime responsibilities and our "Look East Policy". It's only after being appointed to the strategically important Andaman and Nicobar Islands that the full scope and importance of the Indo-Pacific Region (IPR) became clear, for the Andaman Group of Islands lie at the most important junction of South Asia and South East Asia.

Geo Strategic Landscape

The notion of a Pan Asia-Pacific community and of late the term Indo-Pacific region has come to the fore in the last two decades; in my view more to do with rise of the countries of this region and less to do with a competing decline of the powers in the European Theatre. Therefore in my view, the start point of this seminar should be to closely relook at the changing Geo strategic Landscape of this region, its inherent congruence, the historical and emerging rivalries, the increasing desire for "commons" in both economic and strategic/ defence domains and the role of extra regional powers.

Whether the nearly 4 billion people of the IPR be able to realise their dreams of greater prosperity and security for themselves, will depend on myriad factors, some relatively easier to shape, others not so. Is it possible to have common aspirations and is there space for harmonizing competing aspirations is the question that poses itself as we move ahead in the 21st century.

The Role of the Mojor Players in the IPR

While every country is important in its own right, the role that the major players play/will continue to play, and their inter se relationships will largely define the future of this region. China, Japan and India, along with the considerable presence/influence of the USA loom large over this region. The inter-se relationships of this Quartet are complex and shaped by historical legacies, competing interests both economic and strategic, and if I may add a quest for cooperation and balance. Can these large players rise above their individual interests to promote the desirable "Commons". It is this question that will to a large extent determine the way the IPR develops in the future. There are of course other players who are important-South Korea, Vietnam, Indonesia and of course Australia. The seminar could also look at the various regional groupings and how they focus/leverage their strengths and balance their concerns.

The Major Factors of Concern

Cooperation on the challenges of energy, food, health and human resource development are of course the major factors. Providing a better quality of life to the poor and marginalised sections of the society must remain the main focus. The regional comprehensive economic partnership in Phnom Penh last year, has detailed a road map of regional economic integration that can reinforce growth and accelerate development across the region, besides enhancing mutual stakes in regional stability and security. The Indian Prime Minister recently reiterated India's commitment and engagement with the RECP process.

There is a need to invigorate the connectivity corridors in the wider region if we are to develop common interests and stakes. While these connectivity corridors are well defined, there should be a sense of greater urgency in developing both the physical infrastructure and the soft infrastructure.

Along with the land corridors, a stable maritime environment is not only desirable but most essential to promote the right confidence and security for growth of this region. Principles of maritime security need to be affirmed including the right of passage and unimpeded commerce, in accordance with international law and peaceful settlement of maritime disputes.

Threats and Challenges

The IPR faces threats across the spectrum of conflict; ranging from low intensity threats to large scale conventional conflict against a nuclear backdrop. While the possibility of large scale conventional conflict has reduced, these cannot be discounted because of intense rivalries and unresolved territorial and boundary issues between States, which still persist and flare up from time to time. At the higher end there is also a buildup of nuclear capabilities and precision over the horizon weapons. Add to this the dangers of irresponsible states possessing nuclear capabilities and the risk of nuclear technology falling in terrorist hands, make the scenario reasonably scary.

At the lower end of the spectrum, terrorism, piracy and cyber threats are assuming dangerous proportions, and combined with arms and drug smuggling and human trafficking, poses in my view the most immediate and main threat in the region as a whole.

The challenge for policy and capability planners is indeed daunting. Should they plan for a threat that is most likely (sub-conventional), or what is more dangerous i.e the conventional one. The answer is not clear and each nation will have to decide for itself; for example as far as India is concerned, not being part of an alliance or military grouping, has to maintain independent deterrent and response capabilities across the spectrum. How do we reduce the ever increasing burden on defence and security. Apart from resolving the existing disputes through dialogue, the region has to increasingly invest in common and shared responses to tackle threats that spread across national boundaries; the recent anti-piracy effort is a good example.

Disaster Management

The region is prone to major disasters at regular intervals with 70 percent of the occurrences worldwide confined to this region alone. The Tsunami of 2004 and recent cyclones, the floods and recurring earthquakes point to the need for collaborative responses on a multilateral level; the good news is that this is beginning to happen, though much remains to be done.

Role of India in the IPR

By virtue of its location, rising economy, young demographic profile and defence capabilities combined with its pluralistic, democratic and secular profile, India will play an ever increasing and important role in this region, whether it seeks it or not. There are many expectations, obligations and aspirations, many in harmony, but some not, as India strives to define its place on the high table in the region. Very focused on its strategic autonomy, India has to chart a course in harmony with its national interest and that of the region as a whole.

There is a lot of talk of India as a counter balance to China, specially from smaller nations that live under China's ever increasing shadow, and even USA. I personally don't think India is willing to get involved in any such proposition, but would prefer to act as a 'Bridge' or a harmonising influence. The fact is that India realises that China is an important neighbour and trading partner and both the countries have to live in harmony and optimize the relationship for the larger good of the region. Of course there are irritants in this relationship, specially the unresolved border issues and China's support to Pakistan's nuclear programme to name a few, but the sooner these are settled through dialogue, the better for both the countries and the region as a whole. Infact China, the largest country of this region has to develop a more harmonious way of resolving its considerable differences with its neighbours.

India's relationship with Japan, ASEAN and Australia are increasingly becoming important, though they are yet to reach their full potential. Indo-US relations of course are equally important, as are USA's ties with Australia, Japan, Philippines, South Korea and Thailand. The new policy of "US Pivot" to the Asia pacific announced in January 2012 was motivated by the need to respond to the growing assertiveness of some regional powers, as also to reassure its regional allies. How this great game will play out is difficult to guess.

Andaman and Nicobar Islands

Before I end, let me say a few words on the Andaman and Nicobar group of Islands, which I have the honour of representing:

- A grouping of 572 islands and atolls, of which 37 are inhabited; spreading over 750 Kms.

- 1200 Kms from mainland India, but only 100-200 Kms from South East Asia; 30 percent of India's EEZ and marine resources, are around these Islands.

- Dominate the SLOCs passing though Malacca straits.

- Have maintained an ecological focus with 94 percent of the land being forest, reserve forest or mangrove.

- Have a dedicated Tri-Service Command in ANC, whose importance will continue to grow in the future.

Certainly a strategic outpost for India, but can also be a spring board for India's engagement with the rest of the IPR.

I conclude by quoting our Hon'ble Prime Minister at the recently concluded 8th East Asia Summit, and I Quote "We gather in Brunei when the need for collective action, cooperation and collaboration in the Asia Pacific region has never been felt more acutely. Global economic uncertainty and political turmoil in other parts of the world have impacted countries in our region equally. In addition, this vast region faces challenges arising not only from its diversity, but also from differences. Clearly the potential of unprecedented prosperity for our people can be realised only by inculcating a cooperative temper", Unquote.

With this, I come to the end of my inaugural address; I wish your deliberations great success.

Thank you – Jai Hind.

SESSION – I

THE CHANGING GEO-STRATEGIC LANDSCAPE

Chairman	Ambassador Lalit Mansingh, IFS (Retd).
Co-Chairman	Ambassador Gleb A Ivashentsov.
First Paper	Maj Gen BK Sharma, AVSM, SM** (Retd).
Second Paper	Mr Tetsuo Kotani.
Third Paper	Dr Victor V Sumsky.
Fourth Paper	Prof Edward I-Hsin Chen.
Discussion	
Concluding Remarks	Ambassador Lalit Mansingh, IFS (Retd) and Ambassador Gleb A Ivashentsov.

Session - I

Chairman's Opening Remarks

Ambassador Lalit Mansingh, IFS (Retd)

Ambassador Gleb Ivanshentsov, my distinguished co-panelist, Ladies and Gentlemen. Let me congratulate the USI and pay my tribute to the leadership of General PK Singh for having organized this timely seminar.

This is a seminar about the Indo-Pacific region and not the Asia Pacific region. The term Asia Pacific excludes India and therefore gives the feeling that we are not a part of it, and that we are not welcome there. The Indo-Pacific idea puts us where we should belong. We are big stakeholders in the Indo-Pacific region and the region as a whole is a coherent geopolitical entity and is seen as such. One of the most important features of Indian foreign policy in recent times has been the Look East policy. It was launched in 1991 under Prime Minister PV Narasimha Rao. But, the concept of Look East has changed in the last 15 years. The geopolitical scope of this particular region of interest to us expanded from South East Asian region to the East Asian region and now we are looking beyond. Within 15 years, India was accepted as a dialogue partner, became a member of ASEAN forum and eventually, became a member of the East Asia Summit. We are now looking at the membership of Asia Pacific Economic Cooperation (APEC) and Trans Pacific Partnership (TPP). I do not know whether APEC and TPP will accept India as a member right now. I am not even sure whether our leadership is willing to accept the conditions of membership of APEC and TPP.

Also significant in recent times, India's Look East policy has dovetailed into America's pivot towards Asia and rebalance in Asia. Since we have a strategic partnership with the US, the dialogue is proceeding on these lines. Even though we like the term Indo-Pacific and we think we are big stake holders, we are not big players as yet. There are other important stakeholders – US, China, Russia, Japan, South Korea, Australia and many others are coming up. We have to catch up with the geopolitical thinking and find out what other stakeholders are thinking about. So, we have this morning a very distinguished panel of representatives from the stakeholders of this region. Now, I will pass on to my co-panelist Ambassador Gleb Ivanshentsov who would like to say a few words.

Session - I

Co- Chairman's Opening Remarks

Ambassador Gleb A Ivashentsov

I think this seminar is very important and I am happy that I have been invited to take part to express my views here.

We in Russia always consider India as a part of Asia Pacific region. I want to stress that India has been a major player in this area, it is a major player and it is destined to be a major player. This is because India has participated in all main political movements and events of international character in the Asia Pacific whether it is Bandung Conference or Non-Alignment movement. India is a major player and I think all the actors in Asia-Pacific should welcome more active role of India with its democratic tradition. India is introducing democracy in international affairs also at a time when there are attempts by certain powers to dominate the international arena. We are standing for democratic international relations in a multipolar world where all major and smaller countries form a more democratic and secure world.

Session - I

First Paper

Maj Gen BK Sharma, AVSM, SM** (Retd)

Changing Geostrategic Landscape in the
Indo-Pacific Region

"After a decade in which we fought two wars that cost us dearly, in blood and treasure, the United States is turning our attention to the vast potential of the Asia Pacific region...from the Pacific to the Indian Ocean...the United States of America is all in.[1]

Barack Obama,
President of the United States,
17 November 2011.

Introduction

US Secretary of State, Hillary Clinton in her speech titled America's Pacific Century delivered in Hawaii in Nov 2011, described the Asia Pacific region as, "Stretching from the Indian sub-continent to the western shores of America, the region spans two oceans-the Pacific and the Indian that are increasingly linked by shipping and strategy"[2]. General Xiong Guangaki, former Deputy Chief of General staff and Chairman of China Institute of International Strategic Studies at the 3rd meeting of the 2nd Track High Level Dialogue on Sino-US relations, argued that Asia-Pacific generally refers to the region that is best represented by APEC, comprising 21 member countries of the Pacific Rim region[3]. This Chinese interpretation implies exclusion of

---

1 Obama, Remarks by President Obama to the Australian Parliament.

2 Clinton Hillary, remarks at FP's transformational trends forum, http://www. foreign policy. com. 30 Nov 2012.

3 Guangkai X, at the third meeting of at the second meeting of high level dialogue, saisaonline.org, 13 Mar 2012.

Indian Ocean from the lexicon of Asia Pacific. Australia's Defence White Paper, 2013[4] alludes, 'Indo-Pacific' meant "multifaceted globalisation has ensured that developments from the Suez Canal to the Sea of Japan or from African shores of the Indian Ocean to the western Pacific were strongly interrelated and mutually dependent". Indo-Pacific region encompasses almost half of the world population, three of ten largest economies, more than fifth of world GDP, one-third of world exports and half of the world's maritime tonnage. It is home to an enormously populous and diverse mix of ethnicities, cultures, political systems, religions and economies, which further enhances its growing geo-strategic importance. Over the next five years nearly 50 percent of all growth outside the US is expected to come from Asia. The region is the maritime trade highway of the world and joins South East Asian states with the Western Pacific, functioning as the throat of sea routes punctuated by Strait of Malacca, Sunda, Lambok and Makassar. South China Sea (SCS) provides passage to roughly two-third of South Korea's energy supplies, 60 percent of Japan's and Taiwan's, and about 70 percent of China's. SCS and East China Sea (ECS) are rich in fisheries and provide an important source of protein for millions of people, while the seabed is reputed to hold valuable reserves of energy deposits. The emergence of this newly defined area is significant that some observers are now talking of an "Indo-Pacific Pivot."[5] Therefore, the new spatial concept 'Indo-Pacific' could be a useful tool to understand the geopolitics of the 21st century"[6] and analyze the emerging geostrategic shifts. These are elucidated in the succeeding paragraphs.

Geopolitical Trends

Hillary Clinton articulates the importance of the region in these words, "In the next 10 years, we need to be smart and systematic about where we invest time and energy, so that we put ourselves in the best position to sustain our leadership, secure our interests and advance our values. One of the most important tasks of American statecraft over the next decade will therefore be to lock in a substantially increased investment - diplomatic, economic, strategic, and otherwise - in the

---

4 http://en.wikipedia.org/wiki/Indo-Pacific

5 http://thediplomat.com/2013/09/30/india-and-the-rise-of-the-indo-pacific/

6 http://www.icwa.in/crarcfour.html

Asia- Pacific region". She underscores investments by American companies, freedom of navigation in the SCS, countering proliferation efforts of North Korea, and ensuring the transparency in the military activities of the region's key players as the main strategic objectives. The enunciated strategy is marked by six guidelines; strengthening bilateral security alliances, deepening relationship with emerging powers, including with China and Vietnam; engaging with multilateral institutions, expanding trade and investment, forging a broad-based military presence, and advancing democracy and human rights. Treaty alliances with Japan, South Korea, Australia, the Philippines and Thailand are noted as the fulcrum of strategic turn to the Asia–Pacific. There has been a deliberate move to engage with regional groupings. In 2009, the US signed the Treaty of Amity and Cooperation with ASEAN and has increased its participation in groupings such as ASEAN Regional Forum (ARF), APEC and East Asia Summit (EAS). The operational part of the new strategy witnessed innovative rotational deployments of self-sustaining forces, allocation of 60 percent of the air force resources, including tactical aircraft and bomber forces from the continental US and similar percentage of its space and cyber capabilities besides deployment of 60 percent of naval assets in the Western Pacific and Indian Ocean.

China perceives the Asia Pivot Strategy as part of 'Grand Encirclement Design' weaved by the US to contain China. Emboldened by its economic growth, China continues with its ambitious military modernisation programme, thus adding teeth to its 'Counter Intervention Strategy'. As per SIPRI, by the year 2035, if China's economic growth continues, its defense spending will surpass that of the US. China considers Western Pacific vital for its sovereignty, integrity, security and development. The 2008 Defence White paper highlights the importance of "struggle for strategic resources, strategic locations and strategic dominance". In this context, the territorial disputes and consequent military assertion pose a most serious challenge to regional security, with potential to draw the US into the conflict. For geographically restrained China, the security of coastal economic centers of gravity, access to energy, raw materials, export markets and security of SLOCs is critical. The PLAN's counter–piracy missions in the Gulf of Aden and its much-debated 'Malacca Dilemma' underscore the seriousness of Beijing's security concerns along this route. In 2006, president Hu Jintao described the PRC as 'a great maritime power' and urged the transformation of navy from 'near seas active defense' (first group of islands i.e. Kurlie, Taiwan, SCS) to 'far sea defense' (second group of islands from Japan, Guam, northwest Pacific Ocean and even the Indian Ocean. In China's security calculus and 'Two Ocean Strategy', the IOR assumes critical importance. Having successfully developed Hambantota (Sri Lanka), Kyaukphyu (Myanmar) and Gwadar (Pakistan) China is focusing on other ports. Chinese firms are developing Lamu (Kenya), ports in Djibouti, Colombo (Sri Lanka), Chittagong and Sonadia (Bangladesh). These emerging port facilities are described by Booz Allen Hamilton, a known US defence contractor, as "String of Pearls". From Xinjiang, China is developing an economic corridor to the Arabian Sea. The project entails development of Gwadar in the IOR as a petro-chemical hub and construction of Karakoram overland bridge, across Khunjerab pass to Kashgar in Xinjiang province of China. Another strategic transportation corridor being developed by China is from Myanmar to Kunming. In China's calculus, IOR is the arena where India-US-Japan strategic interests coalesce against China and present a formidable threat to Chinese SLOCs, the very lifeline of China's economy. For domination of such a vast area, development of 'Blue Water' maritime capability becomes a strategic imperative. Strategic experts are of the view that it is not long before China's commercial endeavors will assume a military dimension. The emerging developments in the IOR will have a long-term strategic implication for the region.

Indo-Pacific landscape is witnessing yet another emerging shift in Sino-Russian partnership aimed at maintaining a balance of power vis a vis the US. Putin in his recent statement indicated that Russia seeks to integrate its far eastern energy network with East Asia, diversify energy markets, develop East–West land corridor and become a stakeholder in thriving container trade traversing the Indo-Pacific Region. Strategically, Russia seeks to balance the growing influence of the US in its East while safeguarding its Far-East against a rapidly growing China. Also, Russia is becoming growingly conscious of geostrategic importance of the Arctic region and Northern Sea Routes

(NSR) and its impact on the geopolitics of Western SLOCs passing through the Indo-Pacific region. The geopolitics of NSR merits a close watch.

The great power rivalry in the region is widening the division in the ten-member grouping over China's maritime claims in SCS. Broadly, those members with claims in SCS want ASEAN to register serious concerns over what they see as China's belligerent actions to enforce its claims in the waters of SCS and over the Spratly, Parcel and other islands. However, non-claimants, mainly Cambodia supported by Laos and Myanmar, shy to alienate China. They go along with China's insistence on dealing with the issue with each country in turn. China's liberal aid and goodwill in Cambodia, Laos and to a limited extent in Myanmar prevent ASEAN countries to speak in one voice against China's position. Philippines and Vietnam now look openly to America for military and diplomatic support as they face up to an assertive China in their sea of troubles. What shape and course ASEAN takes in the emerging geopolitical milieu remains uncertain?

Economic Trends

As per a forecast carried in the Economist publication titled, "20 Mega Change 50: The World in 2050", by 2040 China's economy would have surpassed that of US. The forecast is based on the assessments of Asian Development Bank (ADB), Carnegie Endowment for International Peace, Goldman Sachs and Pricewaterhouse Cooper. As per Goldman Sachs projections, if US economy grows at 2 percent and China's at 6 percent, China will overtake the US by 2027. The IMF estimates that China will overtake the US by 2017, when the US GDP will be USD 19.70 trillion compared with China's USD 20.33 trillion. According to the Organisation for Economic Cooperation and Development (OECD), China will surpass the United States as the world's largest economy by 2016[7]. In economic terms the region is witnessing increasing economic integration in the form of Regional Free Trade Areas and at the same time competition between the Trans – Pacific Partnership (TPP) and Regional Economic Cooperation Partnership (RECP). The US seeks to benefit from the economic

---

7 http://www.ibtimes.com/oecd-report-says-chinas-economy-will-overtake-us-economy-2016-1146333

dynamism of the region. It has signed Free Trade Agreements with various countries including, Singapore Australia and South Korea. The lynchpin of US economic rebalancing is the TPP - an economic bloc comprising 11 countries, namely US, Chile, New Zealand, Brunei, Singapore, Australia, Peru, Vietnam, Malaysia, Mexico and Canada. With the inclusion of Japan and South Korea in the TPP in the future, it would have a combined GDP of $ 26 trillion i.e., about 40 percent of global GDP and over 30 percent of world exports.

Regional Comprehensive Economic Partnership is a Free Trade Agreement (FTA) scheme of the 10 ASEAN Member States and its FTA Partners (Australia, China, India, Japan, Korea and New Zealand) to be concluded by the end of 2015 includes more than 3 billion people, has a combined GDP of about $17 trillion, and accounts for about 40 percent of world trade. The RCEP takes into account the East Asia Free Trade Agreement (EAFTA) and the Comprehensive Economic Partnership in East Asia (CEPEA) initiatives, with the difference that the RCEP is not working on a pre-determined membership. Instead, it is based on open accession which enables participation of any of the ASEAN FTA partners (China, Korea, Japan, India and Australia-New Zealand) at the outset or later when they are ready to join. Presently, bulk of global trade is conducted in US dollars and more than 60 percent of all global foreign exchange reserves are held in US dollars[8]. The factors such as the US heavy international debtor and China as the second largest economy in the world have sparked a growing discussion among policy makers and academics that the world should no longer rely on a single, dominant currency, such as the dollar. Experts believe that China eventually plans to back the Yuan with gold and try to make it the number one alternative to the US dollar[9].

Trends on Role of Social Media

The civil societies, states and non state actors are increasingly relying on the cyber space and information space in their personal, professional and public activities. These people communicate within

---

8 http://content.time.com/time/world/article/0,8599,1911671,00.html

9 http://www.zerohedge.com/news/2013-10-18/9-signs-china-making-move-against-us-dollar.

and across borders, forming virtual communities that empower citizens at the expense of governments. This virtual space might be called the "interconnected estate" - a place where any person with access to the Internet, regardless of living standard or nationality, is given a voice and the power to effect change. The civil societies in the region have exploited the potential of social media such as Facebook, Twitter, Skype etc. to galvanize civil society movements in the region. "Arab Spring", youth uprising in Turkey and civil society movements in India illustrate the point[10]. Technology geeks are rallying political "flash mobs" that shake repressive governments, building new tools to skirt firewalls and censors, reporting and tweeting the new online journalism, and writing a bill of human rights for the Internet age[11]. Non state actors have effectively used cyber and information space to conceive, plan, coordinate and execute terrorist attacks with masterly skills while remaining physically distant over thousands of miles thus elusive to any detection. While cyber space and digital media have had positive influence in spread of knowledge and promoting commerce and trade, its unbridled use by states and anti-social mafias has aroused a cause of concern. There is a growing demand for declaring cyber and information space as a global common and regulate its use by devising universal protocols and usage norms.

Asymmetric Conflicts

The Indo-Pacific landscape, much like rest of the world, is witnessing pronounced nature of asymmetric conflicts and this trend is bound to grow. A major shift in the domain of warfare is that from concentration of large combat forces in limited battle space or battlefields as seen in the conventional wars to vast spaces in the wilderness and urban centers with small numbers of combatants, mainly non state actors hidden inside them. Therefore, detecting a foe will be more difficult than eliminating him. Detection and destruction of this unidentifiable foe would demand use of precision technologies in electronic intelligence and surveillance and use of precision munitions with satellite guidance to avoid collateral damage. In the arena of

---

10 http://www.economist.com/news/international/21580190-technology-makes-protests-more-likely-not-yet-more-effective-digital-demo.

11 http://www.foreignaffairs.com/articles/66781/eric-schmidt-and-jared-cohen/the-digital-disruption, accessed on 02 Nov 2013.

conventional warfare, the control over resources such as fossilized fuel, rare earth metals and water will be the main driver of intra state and interstate conflicts. The issue of contested sovereignty in the Western Pacific devolves around control over estimated huge deposits of oil and gas, fishing grounds and those in the Middle East (access to headwaters of river Jordan) and South Asia about sharing of water resources between the upper and lower riparian states. The emphasis will shift to use of asymmetric, disruptive stealth technologies and stand off strike capabilities Modern militaries will rely heavily on missiles, submarines, stealth fighter strike aircraft (F35) and UAVs. Lighter and more flexible forces capable of mounting rapid responses will be preferred over heavy and static forces. But relatively weak adversaries, both conventional and sub-conventional, will match strong military capabilities using asymmetric warfare capabilities. Exploitation of cyber space has put a militarily weaker but technically adept adversary on a strong wicket in the art of non - contact warfare. Asymmetric approach in warfare is strongly eroding the strength of a high–end military power[12]. There is a growing trend of Nuclear Weapon States improving their nuclear stockpiles. Declared weapon states like India, Pakistan North Korea are constantly improving their nuclear, weapons, whereas, Iran and Israel, known to have breakout nuclear weapon capability, are showing no signs of capping their Nuke ambitions. Perceived nuclear threats from North Korea by Japan and South Korea on one hand and Saudi Arabia from Iran on the other has triggered the ambition of these countries acquiring Ballistic Missile Defence and nuclear weapons. The unstable nature of regimes in some of the nuclear weapon states and their proximity to non state actors with Jihadi and suicidal mentality are portent with the risk of nuclear weapons or a 'Dirty Bomb' falling in wrong hands and even being used for a nuclear blackmail or terrorist acts.

Conclusion

The geopolitical, economic and security developments in the Indo-Pacific Region have implications for India. India is purportedly projected by the US as a lynchpin of Asia Pivot Strategy and by Japan and ASEAN as a balancer in the region. China is maintaining a close watch on India's role and orientation in the Indo-Pacific Region. India's

---

12 George Friedman and Robert D Kaplan on the Evolution of War, stratfor, 11 Oct 2013.

geostrategic location and rising politico-economic profile provide it a competitive strategic advantage in the Indo-Pacific Region. India's core strategic objectives include becoming the major power in South Asia. Accelerated economic development, securing and protecting energy sources, creation of viable security environment underpin its comprehensive national development and aspiration for global influence, international support and recognition[13]. The Indo-Pacific Region is central to achieving these laudable strategic objectives. It therefore becomes incumbent for India to develop comprehensive national power and master the art of its subtle configuration in keeping with its vital national interests and core strategic objectives in the region. India must remain cognizant of the emerging geostrategic competition in the region and adopt a proactive policy of multiple engagements in sync with its national interests, growing stature and expectations that it evokes from other regional countries.

---

13 Sergei DeSilva-Ranasinghe, India's Strategic Objectives in the Indian Ocean Region, Future Directions International, Perth, 20 October 2011.

Session - I

Second Paper

Mr Tetsuo Kotani

Strategic Landscape: The implication of the East and South China Seas Confrontation

The strategic landscape in Asia is gloomy. The chance for large-scale military conflict is still remote but overlapping territorial claims in the East China Sea and South China Sea can lead to small clashes and escalation. China is the centre of those territorial confrontations. The rise of China is challenging the existing liberal international order in two ways. One is the physical challenge to US military presence and alliance network. The other is the legal challenge to the San Francisco system, which has provided the basis for international order in the post war Asia-Pacific. China's challenge to Japanese control of the Senkaku Islands in the East China Sea is the test of the US-Japan alliance and liberal international order.

Military Balance

The growing Chinese maritime power is changing the military balance in Asia. The stability in Asia long rested on the strategic balance of power among the United States, Japan, Russia, India, and China. The continental power of Russia, India, and China dominated the Asian landmass and the maritime power of the United States and Japan secured freedom of navigation in the Asian littoral. Neither side could project sufficient conventional power into the realm of the other.

However, China's naval modernisation is challenging the US-Japan naval supremacy in the Asian littoral. Given economic interdependence and the need to develop sea power, China has resolved land border disputes with neighbouring countries, including Vietnam and Russia. On the other hand, China is modernizing its naval power to protect its seaborne trade and core maritime interest, Taiwan. To challenge US dominant military power, China's military modernisation focuses on A2/AD.

Primary Chinese A2/AD weaponry includes a large submarine fleet and land-based aircraft carrying anti-ship cruise missiles. Anti-ship ballistic missiles to target moving ships might be added in the near future. A2/AD relies on wide-range ocean surveillance to detect and locate approaching enemy forces. The history of A2/AD is long, although it was called differently in the past. The Imperial Japan adopted the "Gradual Attrition Strategy" during the Pacific War and used submarines and aircraft based on islands under Japanese control to locate and attack US fleet. During the Cold War, the Soviet Union posed a similar threat with long-range aircraft and submarines to locate US naval forces.

China lacks sophisticated ISR capabilities and instead persists in a series of excessive maritime claim, or a legal warfare, as a sea denial strategy. China's domestic law guarantees freedom of navigation in its EEZ but denies the freedom in China's "historic waters." China's EEZ claims are based on the historical "occupation" of the waters in the Yellow Sea, East China Sea, and South China Sea. China thus does not accept surveillance activities by foreign military vessels in its EEZ and fails to recognize the airspace above its EEZ as international airspace. This type of behaviour precipitated the Hainan EP-3 incident in 2001 and the USNS Impeccable incident in 2009.

By claiming the ownership of islets and reefs in the East and South China Seas, China is trying to enhance its ISR capabilities. This Chinese military strategy has stimulated the confrontation over the territories in the Asian waters. In fact, China has occupied several islets and reefs in the South China Sea and constructed military facilities on them, thereby changing the military balance favouring China more. In the East China Sea, China is challenging Japanese control of the Senkaku Islands to enhance its ISR capabilities.

Challenge to the San Francisco System

China is challenging the liberal international order in the Asia-Pacific that has its root in the San Francisco Peace Treaty. The peace treaty legally concluded the Pacific War and formulated the international relations in the region that assumed US forward military presence. However, the peace treaty, signed by 49 countries, failed to prescribe China's position in the system and left unresolved territorial issues.

China is not a party to the San Francisco system, while Taiwan endorsed it. Its relations with the United States and Japan are an outcome of Cold War requirement, not reconciliation. To normalize relations with China, Japan and the United States needed to break off their diplomatic relations with Taiwan. China openly declares the use of force to prevent Taiwanese independence. To prevent US intervention in such a scenario, China is building A2AD capabilities.

As its power grows, China is attempting to create a new international order that favours China. In essence, the rise of China is a challenge to the San Francisco system. Xi Jinping has proposed a new type of great power relations to President Obama. This is a call for US-China accommodation in the Asia-Pacific. This concept assumes mutual respect for core interest or US non-intervention in any conflict over Taiwan or East/South China Sea.

The San Francisco system is a source of unresolved territorial disputes in the South China Sea. Under the peace treaty, Japan gave up all claims over the Paracel and Spratly Islands and there emerged a power vacuum. China started to claim all the land features in the South China Sea based on the nine-dash line and confronted with Vietnam and later with the Philippines. China's claim denies the legitimacy of the peace treaty and by doing so; China is seeking a new order in the South China Sea.

Senkaku and the Future of Asia

By challenging Japan's control of the Senkaku Islands, China is testing the bottom line of Tokyo and strategic position of the Washington. In other words, China is testing the credibility of the US-Japan alliance. Casual observers tend to overlook or underestimate the confrontation between Tokyo and Beijing after Tokyo's purchase of three Senkaku islets in September 2012. It is not merely about the ownership of the small islets in the East China Sea. It is not about territorial or resource nationalism, either. Beijing is challenging the liberal international order after World War II endorsed by the US-Japan alliance. Behind Chinese assertiveness in the East China Seas lies China's A2/AD strategy. The future of Asia rests on the outcome of the strategic competition between the US-Japan alliance and China.

China's claim on the Senkaku lacks legal ground. Its claim is based on historical possession but there is no record of actual control. In short, China discovered the Senkaku Islands in 1971, when Taipei suddenly started to claim the islands, and not in the 15th century. The San Francisco Peace Treaty and the Okinawa Reversion Treaty clearly recognized Japan's ownership of the Senkaku. China is challenging Tokyo over the Senkaku Islands in order to weaken the liberal international order based on the San Francisco system.

The outcome of the current struggle over the Senkakus will have significant implications for the future of the Asia-Pacific. If the confrontation is resolved peacefully, a bright future will be within closer reach for the region. If it is, on the other hand, resolved through coercion, the region is more likely to confront a future defined by Chinese hegemony. And were it to be resolved through war, the region would, of course, face a decidedly dark future.

The military balance in East Asia still favours the United States mainly due to the lack of China's ISR capabilities. But it may not be the case in 2020 or 2030. Also there is always a chance of unexpected accident and escalation. Therefore there is a need to build crisis management and communication with China. However, there is no guarantee that communication with China would work in crisis because China tends to close communication channels in emergency. Remember US-China MMCA could not prevent the EP-3 and Impeccable incidents. China is also reluctant about confidence-building when there is no trust. Crisis management/communication is not a goal but a means to engage China so that it can understand the value and benefit of the preservation of international law and regulations for peaceful resolutions.

Session – I

Third Paper

Dr Victor V Sumsky

The Indo-Pacific Region: A Russian (and Eurasian) Assessment

Before trying to figure out what the term Indo-Pacific Region (IPR) might mean, one has to acknowledge that lately it has become quite popular, if not in all the littoral states, then at least in some of the bigger ones. First and foremost, this is India, and the reason is obvious. Unlike the combination of words that has become so familiar during the last several decades, that is, the Asia-Pacific Region (APR), the name of the IPR sounds like a final confirmation of India's belonging to a group of dynamic Asian nations to its East. Among the other countries that have been actively promoting the IPR formula are Australia, Indonesia, Japan and the United States. China, although not staunchly opposed to this invention, is less enthusiastic.

In Russia the emergence of the IPR discourse has been calmly noticed by some perceptive experts on Asia-Pacific/East Asian affairs but has not produced much reaction beyond their circle.

This lack of excitement is not difficult to explain. After all, the movement towards inter-regional cooperation along the Indo-Pacific lines is not a new phenomenon. It has been in progress at least since the emergence of the ASEAN Regional Forum (ARF, 1994), where a number of South Asian nations got engaged in a multilateral security dialogue with those from the Pacific Rim. In 2005 the launching of the East Asian Summit (EAS) with India as a full-time member consolidated this trend, and five years later the launching of ADMM Plus (which is a meeting of ASEAN Defence Ministers with their counterparts from eight nations who are ASEAN dialogue partners) added a new dimension to it. Thus, no less than three platforms for Indo-Pacific inter-regional discussions and cooperation already exist, and Russia is a participant in all of them.

Once this is taken into account, the IPR may well look, from a Russian point of view, excessive and even irritating – especially because it is provoking a whole string of unanswered questions. For instance, which of the Indian Ocean littoral states to the West of India should be (or should not be) involved in the IPR scheme? Where exactly are its boundaries? Will it extend as far as Iran, or Saudi Arabia, or the countries on the East coast of Africa? Debates on these and related issues have been rather confusing. At present the probability of consensus seems minimal. From that point of view the Indo-Pacific region remains, at best, a matter of future indefinite.

This is not to say, however, that the IPR is just an empty shell, a trendy term with no real meaning and that Russia (which is almost never mentioned as a player of any significance by the IPR pundits) should remain indifferent to its promotion.

A preliminary analysis of what has been published about the IPR leads to a conclusion that, by contrast with the APR, all sorts of economic themes are marginal to this discourse. The real focus is on strategic and security matters, above all on maritime security. The two oceans and the water passages that connect them are described as a huge playground where two rising naval powers, China and India, need to find a mutually acceptable balance between strategic competition and strategic cooperation – and do it in a company of a dominant third power, the United States.

Ideally the IPR looks as a framework in which the three powers should learn to keep their mutual contradictions under control and promote cooperation – for the greater good of themselves and other littoral states. In practice, against the background of American pivot to Asia with all its well-known consequences (like new tensions between China and the US, China and Japan, China and some ASEAN members) it would be natural to suggest that much of the IPR enthusiasm is generated by the urge to contain China.

Is there a chance that an effort like this might actually develop in the IPR framework? Sadly, as far as global adventurism is concerned, nothing seems to be impossible in the early 21st century. However, the probability of genuine success through adventures is a totally different story. In the case of containing China by naval means this probability is not too high, to put it mildly. While the reasons for that are numerous, among the most important ones is the fact that China (like India, by the way) is basically a continental power with a long oceanic coast. Its present geostrategic position is determined not only by the developments on its Southern "waterfront", but by the state of things in its Eurasian "dry land rear". As long as China and Russia continue to cultivate and deepen their strategic trust, attempts to contain China will not work in any meaningful way. As a cure from containment temptations, the reality of Moscow-Beijing cooperation is indirectly but strongly contributing to more prudent strategic scenarios.

Looking at the IPR from a Eurasian angle may lead to some other observations concerning the potential and limitations of the present IPR discourse. When Robert Kaplan describes the IPR as "maritime Eurasia", he actually (although hardly intentionally) encourages that kind of approach.

First, once the IPR is presented in such a way, it starts to look as a part of a bigger whole, and its problems can no longer be isolated from those of Eurasia. Second, since Russia, a continental power with a very long coastline, just like India and China, is the backbone of Eurasia; all sorts of Russian geopolitical and strategic themes become related to the IPR discourse. Third, to Kaplan's description of the IPR one may add a brief comment: Yes, it is "maritime Eurasia", but not the whole of it. How about the huge maritime spaces on Russia's northern and eastern borders? Is not this "maritime Eurasia" too?

These questions and remarks may sound a little abstract until a couple of other questions are posed. Do such quintessential IPR countries as China and India prove by their practical moves that they are looking not just South but North? If China and India are closely interacting with Russia, what are the major reasons?

Development of strong, diversified linkages and a truly strategic partnership with Russia is a lasting and common theme of both the foreign policy of China and that of India. Considering the remaining elements of uneasiness between the two Asian powers, this is quite remarkable in itself. For illustrations, just look at such formats as RIC and BRICS, at the SCO which is there for the sake of protecting the common security of Central Asia and the states that are bordering on it. The recently articulated desire of both China and India to have a presence in the Arctic area of "maritime Eurasia" and to share in its development may open a totally new (and hopefully, quite promising) chapter in the story of interactions between these two powers and Russia.

Stable access to an enormous variety and amount of resources is a must for China and India if they are to continue to modernise and function as engines of Asian and, to an even greater extent, global growth. Here Russia, especially that part of it which lies beyond the Urals, has a lot to offer, with an ultimate aim of boosting its own prosperity and progress, of course. The need for greater infrastructural, technological and institutional connectivity between the three powers in order to extract, process and transport these resources, and then to market the processed goods may lead to the implementation of veritable mega-projects, bringing today's Eurasia to a totally new level of integration and development, a level more worthy of Eurasia's well-known description as the geopolitical centre of the world.

If this happens, will it mean that Eurasia is eclipsing what we call today East Asia, or APR, or IPR in terms of strategic importance and economic dynamism? No, because China and India will belong to both of these realms. As for Russia, its sustained cooperation with China and India may bring it into a position in which it will be a much better economic partner for other Asian nations and a stronger contributor to regional stability.

Getting back to the IPR concept as we know it today, let me point to what I see as its primary weakness. Roughly speaking, the whole IPR discourse is inspired by one particular aspect of regional reality, namely, intensifying strategic competition between great powers, with a tendency to reduce even that phenomenon to their naval competition and, by implication, to reduce such highly complicated geopolitical entities as China and India to just emerging naval powers. If this is true then the concept that we are discussing lacks depth and lacks it badly.

To add depth to it, it is not enough to say in passing that the IPR is "maritime Eurasia". It is essential to analyze the potential implications of this statement. If such analysis is not done, then, paradoxically, the statement itself becomes invalid. In this case the IPR turns into nothing more than "the maritime underbelly of Eurasia". This is how a distinguished Indian colleague referred to it in a private conversation with me, and this is what it is today, at least, in our common opinion.

Does Russia have an alternative vision for the region, or at least an alternative name? It looks like it does, judging by the volume published in Moscow in 2010 by a group of scholars from MGIMO University where I work at present. The title of the book is "Big East Asia: World Politics and Regional Transformations", the editor is Professor Alexei Voskresensky, a well-known authority on problems of contemporary Asia. Big East Asia stands for the emerging macro-region comprising Northeast Asia, Southeast Asia, South Asia (up to the western borders of India), Central Asia and Russia. What we see here is the combination of China, India and Russia seeking closer ties between themselves and other Eurasian neighbours for the sake of regional peace, security and development. This is basically the kind of cooperation framework which has been attempted to be outlined in this paper.

Session – I

Fourth Paper

Prof. Edward I-Hsin Chen

Taiwan's Perspective of the US Rebalancing Asia Policy

Introduction

US Secretary of State, Hillary Rodman Clinton, claimed "the US is back (to Asia)" in Bangkok on 21 July 2009.[1] However, it was not until November 2011 that President Barack Obama really returned to Asia with support of economic initiatives, democratic political values, diplomatic resolve, and military strength.

Most countries have been caught up in the sovereignty and energy disputes in the East China Sea and South China, in the contest between China's soft power and US's "smart power," and in a subtle rivalry between the China-led Regional Comprehensive Economic Partnership (RCEP) and US-led Trans-Pacific Partnership (TPP).

This paper will scrutinize how Taiwan has benefited from the US Rebalancing Asia policy in political, military, strategic, diplomatic, Cross-Strait, and economic dimensions.

Taiwan as a Symbol of Democracy

Taiwan has developed into a vibrant democracy, holding regular, free, and fair elections since mid-1980s. Now Taiwan is recognized around the world as a model for both economic development and democratic reform.[2]

---

1 Hillary Rodham Clinton, Remarks With Thai Deputy Prime Minister Korbsak Sabhavasu, Secretary of State, Government, House, Bangkok, Thailand, July 21, 2009, available at http://www.state.gov/secretary/rm/2009a /july/126271.htm, accessed 24 July 2009.

2 State's Moy on Trends in US-Taiwan Relationship, Remarks by Kin Moy, Deputy Assistant Secretary, Bureau of East Asian and Pacific Affairs, Carnegie Endowment for

Washington's promotion of democracy, freedom, and human rights in the Asia-Pacific region has also benefited Taiwan's position. In the eyes of Washington, Taiwan is a democracy showing respect towards public opinion in spite of some defects, whereas China's one-party government system is less reliable, less stable, and less transparent than the democratic system.

Political systems matter in international relations. The United States and Chinese political systems are mutually exclusive in nature.[3] And it is the main reason why the United States and China will never evolve from two competitive powers into a pair of complex interdependent states despite more than ninety communication channels between them.[4]

There are three dimensions of Taiwan's democracy i.e. a values system; a way of life; and a process. First, democracy in Taiwan is a prevailing value system that no one dares to challenge such a value system. The government sets the agenda for state's policies, whereas public opinion dominates the course of most of the policies. The public opinion is so strong that the cabinet is shaky anytime. It is so strong that many officials are ready to resign every day.

Certainly, there are merits of democracy in Taiwan as a value system. The first of them is that while democracy may be reversed in different forms in many third world countries whereas Taiwan's democracy is irreversible. The second is that any political leader in Taiwan cannot violate the mainstream value or his or her popularity or supporting rate will be in decline. The third is that any attempt to change Taiwan's legal status requires the overwhelming majority of Taiwan people's consent. The fourth is that the United States might

---

International Peace, Washington DC, 03 October 2013, available at http://translations. state.gov/st/english/texttrans/2013/10/20131003284024.html, accessed 06 October 2013.

3 Kenneth Lieberthal and Wang Jisi, *Addressing US-China Strategic Distrust* (Washington: D.C.: John L. Thornton China Center at Brookings, 2012), Monograph Series, No. 04, March 2012.

4 The concept of a pair of complex interdependent states, judged by three criteria, namely, the number of channels of communication, no priority of agenda setting, and no hostility or military threat, was first proposed by Robert O. Keohane and Joseph S. Nye, Jr., see their *Power and Interdependence* (New York: Harper Collins Publishers, 1989), 24-29, 249-250 & 255-257.

not be interested in helping to defend an authoritarian Taiwan in times when it formed a loose anti-Soviet alliance with China, Japan, and West Europe during the Cold War era. Since Taiwan started to democratize itself in 1986, however, the United States cannot simply afford to lose a democratic Taiwan.

Nevertheless, democracy in Taiwan as a value system also contains defects. The first of them is that Taiwan's identity is too strong to tolerate any different identity. The second is that Taiwan's democracy has turned out to be a populist democracy. The third is that Taiwan's democracy as a value system does not contain some necessary elements such as constitutionalism and rule of law to set norms and regulations of a democratic society.

Second, democracy in Taiwan has turned out to be a way of life. When democracy has become a way of life, it helps explain why the overwhelming majority of people prefer to maintain the status quo. It also suggests that when Taiwan people get accustomed to democracy as a way of their daily life, they will be reluctant to accept unification.

Certainly, there are merits of democracy in Taiwan as a way of life. The first of them is that when democracy has become a way of life, Taiwan's democracy cannot be reserved. The second is that any political leader will not attempt to change democracy as a way of life or his popularity or supporting rate will be in decline. The third is that when democracy has become a way of life, any attempt to change Taiwan's legal status will become extremely difficult, if not impossible. The fourth is that when democracy has become a way of life, the United States must show its like-mindedness to safeguard Taiwan's democracy.

Nevertheless, democracy in Taiwan as a way of life also contains defects. The first of them is that democracy in Taiwan as a way of life hinders Taiwan society from reaching consensus on many economic issues such as Economic Cooperation Framework Agreement (ECFA), and much less on more politically sensitive issues. The second is that Taiwan's democracy as a way of life has turned out to be a populist democracy which is sometimes violent. The third is that Taiwan's democracy as a way of life does not contain elements such as showing respect to pluralistic cultures and tolerance towards different ideas.

Third, democracy in Taiwan has become a process on any specific issue. As President George W Bush pointed out during his transit to China via Japan in November 2005, "Modern Taiwan is free and democratic and prosperous. By embracing freedom at all levels, Taiwan has delivered prosperity to its people and created a free and democratic Chinese society."[5]

When democracy has become a process itself, it partly explains why the *status quo* has become the top choice of Taiwan people. It also suggests that when Taiwan people get accustomed to democracy as a process, unification can hardly become their preferred choice.

Certainly, there are merits of democracy in Taiwan as a process. The first of them is that when democracy has become a process, any attempt to overthrow the democracy will not be approved in the process of referenda voting. The second is that any political leader will not attempt to reject referenda voting as a process of public opinion's expression or his popularity will be in decline. At least, political leaders will pretend to embrace referenda voting so that they do not lose votes. The third is that when democracy has turned out to become a process, any attempt to change Taiwan's legal status will become extremely difficult, if not impossible. The fourth is that when democracy has become a process, the United States must show its political will to safeguard Taiwan's democracy by not allowing any third party to disrupt such a process.

Nevertheless, democracy in Taiwan as a process also contains defects. The first of them is that democracy in Taiwan as a process will hinder Taiwan society from reaching consensus on many economic issues such as the Service Trade Agreement, not to mention more politically sensitive issues. The second is that Taiwan's democracy as a process has turned out to be a populist democracy which is sometimes violent. The third is that Taiwan's democracy as a way of life does not contain some necessary elements such as civic culture and to-give-and-to-take mutually compromising culture.

There are political implications of democracy in Taiwan as a value system, a way of life, and a process for China-Taiwan-US

---

5 Terence Hunt, "Bush Urges Greater Freedom in China; Speech Cites Taiwan's Success as Democracy," *Associated Press*, 16 November 2005.

relations. The first of them is that Taiwan's achievement in democracy has proved it is standing on the right side of the history of human beings. Therefore, Taiwan's democracy, even though it is reachable in China today, can be set a long-term goal for Chinese people as well as Chinese leaders. In his transit to China via Japan in November 2005, President George W Bush prodded China to grant more political freedom to its 1.3 billion people and held up archrival Taiwan as a society that successfully moved from repression to democracy as it opened its economy. Bush suggested China should follow Taiwan's path.[6] The second is that a too strong public opinion and populist democracy in Taiwan will scare away Chinese leaders to press ahead with their next-step democratization program. The third is that no matter whether Washington adopts an ambiguous strategy or a clarified strategy in the Taiwan Strait, China fully understands that one of the roles the US is playing is safeguarding Taiwan's democracy by means of US presence in the Asia-Pacific region.

In safeguarding Taiwan's democracy as a value system, a way of life, and a process, the United States could play a decisive, significant, and sometimes, multidimensional role.[7] For example, Washington could continue to play the role of a supervisor overseeing no use of force across the Taiwan Strait and ensuring compliance with the cross-Strait agreements. Whenever there is a controversy over the implementation of agreements across the Strait, the United States could ask both sides to set self-restraint, thus playing the role of an arbitrator. Most importantly, it could play the role of a guarantor by honouring the TRA as well as maintaining its security commitment and arms sales to Taiwan.

Therefore, the three dimensions of Taiwan's democracy, namely, a value system, a way of life, and a process, are the status quo the overwhelming majority of Taiwan people want to preserve most. Taiwan sets a positive example of a stable democracy to China and other Asian countries. In contrast to China's non-transparent one-party system, Taiwan is a beacon of democracy in the region. In safeguarding

---

6 *Ibid.*

7 Edward I-hsin Chen, "US Role in Future Taipei-Beijing Relations," King-Yuh Chang, ed., *Political and Economic Security in Asia-Pacific* (Taipei: Great Mountain Publisher, 2004), 82-95.

Taiwan's democracy, the US could play a multidimensional role as a promoter, an arbitrator, a guarantor, and a supervisor.

American strategic objectives lie in ensuring Taiwan remains a secure democratic state in the region, for losing Taiwan's democratic symbol would be a major setback to American soft power in the Asia-Pacific.

US Arms Sales Increased

China's objective is to be in a position to settle sovereignty disputes on its own terms. To achieve this objective, China is increasing its military budget and developing capabilities to deter, delay, or deny possible US support for Taiwan in the event of conflict.[8] Today, not only does the balance of military power across the Strait tilt in favour of China, but China's anti-access military capability is also growing more capable of denying the US access to the region's oceans in the event of a future conflict. Both Washington and Taipei increasingly tend to believe that China is aggressive and ambitious in nature.[9] China's military rise has changed the balance of power across the Taiwan Strait, putting Taiwan's ability to come to the political table with any leverage into jeopardy.

In order to reach this objective, China has increased its military budget and is developing capabilities to deter, delay, or deny possible US support for Taiwan in the event of conflict, thereby causing suspicion from the United States in particular as to what China's strategic intention would be. Not only the balance of military power across the Strait continues to tilt in favour of China, but also China's military capabilities have upgraded from a status that made US deterrence more complicated than before into a status that could deter US deterrence by means of its anti-access strategy.

While the United States keeps a close eye on the progress achieved in cross-Taiwan Strait relations in recent years and encourages both

---

8 Edward I-hsin Chen, "The Security Dilemma in US-Taiwan Informal Alliance Politics," *Issues & Studies*, Vol. 48, No. 1, March 2012, 1-50

9 US Defense Department, *Military and Security Development Involving the People's Republic of China 2011* (Washington, DC: Create Space, 2011), available at http://www.defense.gov/pubs/2011_CMPR_Final.pdf, accessed 01 May, 2011.

sides to continue these efforts, the strong US-Taiwan security partnership has provided the security and confidence necessary for improvements in cross strait ties, reiterating US opposition to the use of intimidation or coercion to resolve differences.[10]

A speech on US policy at a dinner for the US-Taiwan Defence Industry Conference in Annapolis, Maryland from 29 September to 01 October 2013 reiterated that the United States will continue its commitment to Taiwan's security and that Taiwan is an important security partner for the United States.[11] According to him, the core purpose of the strategic partnership between Washington and Taipei is to ensure that Taiwan is free from threats and coercion, stressing that it was necessary to ensure peace and stability in the Taiwan Strait and in the Asia-Pacific region.

In light of this strategic imbalance and possible China's use of force against Taiwan, the Obama administration has significantly increased its arms sales to Taiwan since 2009, believing that doing so would not only help Taiwan defend itself but also strengthen Taipei's confidence in negotiating with Beijing. Although these arms sales are a far cry from equalizing the military imbalance, they have been a significant boon to Taiwan's security position and have caused China to more seriously weigh the costs of any invasion scenario.

Taiwan's Value as a Strategic Partner Affirmed

As part of its rebalancing policy in Asia, the Obama administration sought to strengthen its relationship with its allies and to engage with new partners in the Asia-Pacific region. Consequently, Taiwan's value as a strategic partner in Asia has significantly increased.

In a speech at the East-West Center of Hawaii University on 10 November 2011, Hillary Clinton pointed out that while "we will

---

10 State's Moy on Trends in US-Taiwan Relationship, Remarks by Kin Moy, Deputy Assistant Secretary, Bureau of East Asian and Pacific Affairs, Carnegie Endowment for International Peace, Washington, DC, 03 October 2013, available at http://translations.state.gov/st/english/texttrans/2013/10/20131003284024.html, accessed 06 October 2013.

11 William Lowther, "US Wants A Strong Taiwan 'Free from Threat': US Official," *Taipei Times,* 03 October 2013, available at <http://www.taipeitimes.com/News/taiwan/archives/2013/10/03/2003573587>; and CAN, "Taiwan Presses US for Advanced Fighters, Submarines," *The China Post,* 03 October 2013, <http://www.wantchinatimes.com/news-subclass-cnt.aspx?id=20131002000059&cid=1101>.

remain committed to the one-China policy and the preservation of peace and stability across the Taiwan Strait, she emphasized, "We have a strong relationship with Taiwan, an important security and economic partner, and we applaud the progress that we have seen in Cross-Strait relations between China and Taiwan…and we look forward to continued improvement so there can be peaceful resolution of their differences."[12]

In a speech at Carnegie Endowment for International Peace, Washington, DC, on 03 October 2013, Kin Moy, Deputy Assistant Secretary, Bureau of East Asian and Pacific Affairs, praised the "comprehensive, durable, mutually beneficial relationship" between the United States and Taiwan.[13] Other than "an important security and economic partner," Taiwan's status is upgraded to "comprehensive, durable, mutually beneficial partner."

American commitments to its allies and partners in the Asia-Pacific region are not easily broken. For example, if Washington was to abandon any of its allies and partners in the region, Asia-Pacific countries would be shocked, and the damage done to the perception of American power abroad would be huge. As a result, Taiwan's fear of American abandonment has been significantly reduced since 2011 and its confidence in the American security umbrella has increased.

Taiwan is Relieved from China's Pressure for Political Talks

The US pivot has eased pressure on Taiwan to engage China in political talks about reunification. Although Cross-Strait relations have improved recently, most people in Taiwan prefer to maintain the status quo. Nonetheless, since the inking of ECFA and related follow-up agreements, China has constantly promoted Cross-Strait political talks.

In 2010, a number of China's actions were perceived by many

---

12 Hillary Rodham Clinton, Secretary of State, "America's Pacific Century," A speech at East-West Center, Honolulu, HI, 10 November 2011, available at http://www.state.gov/secretary/rm/2011/11/176999.htm, accessed 13 November 2011.

13 State's Moy on Trends in US-Taiwan Relationship, Remarks by Kin Moy, Deputy Assistant Secretary, Bureau of East Asian and Pacific Affairs, Carnegie Endowment for International Peace, Washington, DC, 03 October 2013, available at http://translations.state.gov/st/english/texttrans/2013/10/20131003284024.html, accessed 06 October 2013.

as overly aggressive. In addition to designating Taiwan, Tibet, and its new territories (Xingjian) as parts of Beijing's "core interests," China flexed its muscle along its peripheral seas and adopted an assertive attitude in territorial disputes with its neighbours. China's assertiveness and its implicit/explicit claims of "core interests" over Taiwan, the Yellow Sea, the East Sea, and the South China Sea have contributed to the strategic distrust between the United States and China.[14] China's actions were not ignored by the Obama administration, which responded by taking the initiative and stressing its rebalancing Asia policy.[15]

Amidst this great power rivalry, it is prudent for Taiwan to maintain a balance between relying on US security commitments on the one hand and China's economy and market on the other. In fact, this orientation is common practice among many of China's neighbouring states, including Japan, South Korea, the Philippines, Vietnam, Thailand, Indonesia, and Singapore.

Taiwan is in a difficult position, however. In the face of China's growing pressure for progress on cross-Strait political talks, Taipei cannot fully reject Beijing's overtures after taking so many benefits from China, but Taipei must also satisfy domestic mainstream public opinion which prefers the status quo. Fortunately, US policy has helped to relieve Taipei from Beijing's pressure for political talks by: restating America's strong support for the peaceful resolution of the cross-Strait tensions; redirecting China's attention from Taiwan's political status to America's diplomatic, economic, military, and political presence in the Asia-Pacific region; pressuring China on its domestic human rights record; affirming Taiwan's value as a strategic, economic and security partner; and increasing Taiwan's negotiating position through arms sales.[16]

---

14 Kenneth Lieberthal and Wang Jisi, *Addressing US-China Strategic Distrust* (Washington: D.C.: John L. Thornton China Center at Brookings, 2012), Monograph Series, No. 4, March 2012.

15 Jeffrey A. Bader, *Obama and China's Rise: An Insider's Account of America's Asia Strategy* (Washington, DC: Brookings Institution Press, 2012), 69-82.

16 Due in part to increased confidence from US arms sales, the Kuomintang's Honorary chairman, Wu Po-Hsiung, proposed the "One China Framework" when he met Xi Jinping, General Secretary of the Communist Party of China, in Beijing on 14 June 2013, launching

Taiwan's International Presence Expanded

US rebalancing policy has helped Taiwan to develop a model for increasing its international presence. So far, this model has significantly been applied in the Taiwan-Japan fishing agreement and will be put to the test in the recent Taiwan-Philippines conflict.

Following Japan's nationalization of the Diaoyutai islands in September 2012, Taiwan confronted Japan about its territorial claims. While Beijing called for Cross-Strait cooperation in tackling the Diaoyutai disputes with Japan, Washington kept a close eye on how Taipei would respond. After Taiwan rejected cross-Strait cooperation on the Japanese issue, the United States decided to exert pressure on Japan for Tokyo's concession on Taiwanese fishing rights. American support provided the critical breakthrough the Ma Ying-jeou administration had worked for during sixteen rounds of talks within the past seventeen years to achieve.

A similar incident occurred in May 2013 when a Taiwanese fishing boat captain was shot at by a coast guard vessel of the Philippines. A verbal confrontation between Taipei and Manila soon escalated when Taiwan dispatched its coast guard and naval vessels to safeguard its fishing boats in the disputed waters. An investigation was conducted to determine responsibility for the tragedy. Following Taiwan's rejection of China's calls for Cross-Strait negotiations on this issue, the United States intervened and pressured the Philippines for Manila's apology and concessions for Taiwanese fishing rights in the controversial waters.

In a speech on US-Taiwan relations at the Washington-based Carnegie Endowment for International Peace, Kin Moy, Deputy Assistant Secretary of State for East Asian and Pacific affairs, cited the agreement signed between Taiwan and Japan in April 2013 on fishing in the East China Sea as an example of Taiwan's efforts to work "peacefully and constructively with its neighbours to manage and resolve disputes." Another example, he said, is the resolution of a dispute with the Philippines over an altercation between the Philippine

---

a new round of political talks across the Strait.

coast guard and a Taiwan fishing vessel.[17]

According to him, the United States welcomes cooperative dispute resolution, reducing tensions through dialogue, and promoting peace and stability in the region. It is US's belief that dispute resolution helps establishes procedures which reduce the likelihood of future miscalculations or unwanted, harmful confrontations.

On Taiwan's bid to participate meaningfully in international Organisations, such participation represents an important acknowledgment of Taiwan's status as a positive and responsible contributor to the international community. The United States fully supports Taiwan's membership in intergovernmental Organisations where statehood is not a requirement, and encourages Taiwan's meaningful participation in Organisations where its membership is not possible.[18]

With the US's support, Taiwan has participated as an observer in the World Health Organisation and in the 38th International Civil Aviation Organisation (ICAO) Assembly as a guest of ICAO Council President Roberto Kobeh González.[19] Taiwan's participation was arranged through international dialogue and cooperation. In fact, Beijing was reluctant to extend its assistance to Taipei in this regard in the beginning, believing that there was no urgent need for Taiwan to become a part of the ICAO. It was not until President Obama signed the bill approved by both houses of US Congress that China was forced to take into serious consideration, Taiwan's participation in the ICAO to make up its earlier inaction. In other words, in the absence of US's initiative, China would not move at all. The active participation of Taiwan's delegation not only supports ICAO's mission

---

17 State's Moy on Trends in US-Taiwan Relationship, Remarks by Kin Moy, Deputy Assistant Secretary, Bureau of East Asian and Pacific Affairs, Carnegie Endowment for International Peace, Carnegie Endowment for International Peace, 03 October 2013, available at http://translations.state.gov/st/english/texttrans/2013/10/20131003284024.html, accessed 06 October 2013.

18 *Ibid.*

19 Taiwan's Participation in the International Civil Aviation Organisation (ICAO), Jen Psaki, Department Spokesperson, Office of the Spokesperson, Washington DC, 24 September 2013, available at http://www.state.gov/r/pa/prs/ps/2013/09/214658.htm, accessed 27 September 2013.

to promote global aviation safety and security but also strengthens the ICAO as an institution.

American support has allowed Taiwan to successfully promote its national interests, increase its international presence and publicity, and expand its fishing rights in both East China Sea and South China Sea.

Taiwan Deserves an Opportunity to Join the TPP

Last but not least, the US pivot policy provides Taipei a better chance of joining the TPP. Immediately after his return from the APEC meet in September 2012, Lien Chan, former ROC Vice President and Special Envoy to APEC, disclosed that the Obama administration may welcome Taiwan to join the TPP.

The TPP is considered an important move toward the Free Trade Area of the Asian-Pacific (FTAAP).[20] President Obama announced at the APEC Summit that the United States will play a leading role in promoting the TPP in the Asia-Pacific region. His call for the establishment of the TPP in the region was echoed by Japan, Canada and Mexico.[21]

President Ma responded by saying that Taiwan would join the US-led Asian economic bloc within ten years while it completes preparations to reshuffle its domestic economic structure. When Raymond Burghardt, Chairman of the American Institute in Taiwan, paid a visit to Taipei on 31 January 2012, he linked the bilateral trade dispute to Taiwan's overall trade liberalization and its engagement with regional trade partners. He pointed out that, "Taiwan needs to have better relations with the Asia-Pacific region beyond China. Taiwan has said it has interests in joining the TPP in 10 years. Why wait 10 years? Why not make it sooner?"[22]

20Remarks by the President to CEO Business Summit in Yokohama, Japan, Office of the Press Secretary, The White House, 12 November 2010, available at http://www.whitehouse.gov/the-press-office/2010/11/12/remarks-president-ceo-business-summit-yokohama-japan, accessed 15 November 2010.

21 Remarks by President Obama and Prime Minister Kan of Japan in Statements to the Press in Yokohama, Japan, Office of the Press Secretary, The White House, 13 November 2010, available at http://www.whitehouse.gov/the-press-office/2010/11/13/remarks-president-obama-and-prime-minister-kan-japan-statements-press-yo, accessed 16 November 2010.

22 Shih Hsiu-chuan, "AIT Chairman Links Beef to Trade Talks and TPP Accession,"

The more FTAs that Taiwan accumulates, the more likely it will gain support from the United States to join the TPP. For example, Taiwan has signed an economic partnership agreement with New Zealand (ATNZEP) and is very close to the inking of a similar agreement with Singapore (ATSEP), improving its chances to become a TPP signatory. As an important security and economic partner of the United States, Taiwan deserves an opportunity to join the TPP.

The United States has always told Taiwan that any TPP candidate must be willing to adopt the high standards and ambitious commitments of TPP. It is focused on concluding the agreement among the twelve current TPP partners. It is also developing the TPP to potentially include other regional economies, noting that existing TPP partners must approve by consensus the addition of new partners.[23]

Since 1994, the Trade and Investment Framework Agreement (TIFA) has been the main channel for dialogue strengthening bilateral trade and investment links between Taiwan and the United States. Nonetheless, Taiwan has now taken into serious consideration its participation in the TPP for several reasons.

First, if Taiwan continues to negotiate with the United States under TIFA, such talks would not only hurt the relationship between the ruling party and the opposition party on the one hand and the government and the people on the other but also damage the relationship between Taiwan and the United States. In a recent speech in Taiwan, Dr Kurt Campbell, former US assistant secretary of state for East Asian and Pacific affairs, pointed out: "There has to be

---

Taipei Times (Taipei), 01 February 2012, 2, http://www.taipeitimes.com/News/taiwan/archives/2012/02/01/2003524404; "MOEA Trying to Resolve US Beef Row," *The China Post* (Taipei), 01 February 2012, http://www.Chinapost.com.tw/taiwan/foreign-affairs/2012/02/01/330283/MOEA-trying.htm. But Burghardt added that "there are a lot of things Taiwan would have to do with its agriculture policy, its policy in the pharmaceutical and financial sectors. All of these things have to be liberalized."

23 State's Moy on Trends in US-Taiwan Relationship, Remarks by Kin Moy, Deputy Assistant Secretary, Bureau of East Asian and Pacific Affairs, Carnegie Endowment for International Peace, Carnegie Endowment for International Peace, 03 October 2013, available at http://translations.state.gov/st/english/texttrans/2013/10/20131003284024.html, accessed 06 October 2013.

political ambition and that has to extend beyond one political party."[24] However, controversial trade issue would only cause a shut-down between the ruling party and the opposition party in Taiwan. The US beef issue resulted in a partial reshuffling with the ROC government during the period from 2009 to 2001, resulting in the stepping-down of several high-level officials, much less the more controversial US pork issue.

In other words, Taiwan has been tired of utilizing the TIFA process to negotiate with the United States on their bilateral trade issues as past experience proves that such a prolonged process is only a disaster to Taiwan.

Second, it goes without saying that Taiwan's economic and trade liberalization lags behind the United States, Japan, Canada, Australia, New Zealand and Singapore. However, Taiwan is not next to any other country in the TPP. If Vietnam, Brunei, Malaysia, Mexico, Chile, and Peru could join the TPP, there is no reason in the eyes of the overwhelming majority of Taiwan people that Taiwan cannot be part of the TPP.

Third, in the wake of president Obama's absence in the APEC and EAS summits, China gains the upper hand over the United States in the economic and trade realms in the Asia-Pacific. Therefore, the Obama administration must make a right strategic choice before it is too late. It would be prudent for the United States to encourage its economically better-off allies and partners like Indonesia, Thailand, and Taiwan to follow the "Japan model," namely, join first, negotiate later, and honour commitment finally. Doing so would not only help the United States to reverse its disadvantageous position in the subtle rivalry between the China-led RCEP and US-led TPP but would also help Washington to realise its target of increasing its trade volume in the Asia-Pacific, thereby creating a win-win scenario between the United States and its trading partners in the region.

---

24 CNA, "Taiwan Needs Ambition to Join TPP: Former US Official," *The China Post*, 16 October 2013, http://chinapost.com.tw/taiwan/foreign-affairs/2013/10/16/391417/Taiwan-needs.htm; and Shih Hsiu-chuan, "Taiwan Needs to Diversify Across Region: Campbell," *Taipei Times*, 16 October 2013, 1, http://www.taipeitimes.com/News/front/archives/2013/10/16/2003574614.

Conclusion

Taiwan has developed into a vibrant democracy, holding regular, free, and fair elections since mid-1980s. Now Taiwan is recognized around the world as a model for both economic development and democratic reform. The three dimensions of Taiwan's democracy, namely, a value system, a way of life, and a process, are the *status quo* the overwhelming majority of Taiwan people want to preserve most. In safeguarding Taiwan's democracy, the United States will continue to play a multidimensional role: promoter, arbitrator, guarantor, and supervisor.

Washington's promotion of democracy, freedom and human rights in the Asian-Pacific region has benefited Taiwan's position. As a result of increased US activity in the region, Taiwan was supported as a strategic democracy, received arms sales from the United States, was affirmed as an important security and economic partner or a comprehensive, durable, and mutually beneficial partner, was relieved from China's political pressures, expanded its international presence, and improved its chances of joining the TPP.

Taiwan will in turn contribute to the peace, prosperity, and stability in the Asia-Pacific region by further improving its relations with the states in the region, and China and the United States in particular.

Although Taiwan has benefited greatly from the US pivot to Asia, Taiwan, as a democracy, has to rely more on its own in the future while welcoming the support from other states.

Session - I

Discussion

Issue Raised

Don't you think the word 'fence sitters' is a bit too strong for nations like Malaysia and Indonesia? They are bridge builders and mediators in the region which makes their presence less visible.

Response

I respect your observation. We can use the word 'strategic balancers' for them instead of 'fence sitters'. Indonesia and Malaysia are important nations. They need to be more pro-active in their approach and not let the US or China hijack the agenda. We want to see path breaking initiatives from these nations.

Issue Raised

Can we exclude Pakistan from the Indo-Pacific region?

Response

India holds no veto on anybody's participation in any region. Pakistan is a member of the region and SAARC as well. Should it be interested in the IPR, it should apply to APEC and EAS. If other member states agree to its membership, it should get it.

Issue Raised

Will Japan risk a war with China over Senkaku islands?

Response

Yes of course. We are trying to establish a crisis management mechanism to avoid war. If China attacks Japanese territory, we have to exercise self defence. So, we are preparing for a crisis mechanism and eventuality for war as well.

Issue Raised

China has border issues with most of its neighbours. Would China risk a war against Japan due to the present geopolitical situation?

Response

China is not ready for the war at the moment as the military balance clearly favours US-Japan in the South China Sea. China wants to buy time for a favourable military balance. China will never give up Senkaku islands. Small incidents can escalate and we are preparing for that.

Issue Raised

What can Russia offer to the Indo Pacific Region?

Response

Russia has never been more open to the world than it is now. Russia has acknowledged the importance of Asia. There are signs of that happening. Russia is a Eurasian power and has to look both ways.

Issue Raised

Is adhering to democracy a prerequisite for peace in the Indo Pacific Region?

Response

Democracy as practiced in one nation cannot be mechanically imposed on other nations. It will be an area of quarrels and disputes. The region should have democracy without external considerations.

Issue Raised

IPR is region where nuclear arsenals are being increased. New nations are trying for nuclear weapons. Will the allies tell the US to reduce the salience of nuclear weapons in the region so that US-China tension can be reduced?

Response

Nuclear weapons play an important role in today's world. I am not sure even if the US tries to reduce its nuclear capabilities, China will follow suit. It may try to increase its nuclear arsenal and try to reach parity with the US.

Issue Raised

Russia should break its isolation and take more active interest in the Indo-Pacific region especially the IOR.

Response

I disagree that Russia is getting isolated in the IPR. Russia acknowledges that Asia is becoming important. Russia too has undergone great transformation and the Asian Policy of Russia is to look in both directions i.e. Asia as well as Europe. But, yes Russia has to increase its attention towards Asia.

Session - I

Chairman's Concluding Remarks

Ambassador Lalit Mansingh

Thank you Ambassador. I think that should be the outlook for our discussions focusing on an inclusive collaboration of stakeholders and not an exclusive one. To have democratic international relations to quote the Ambassador, to have a multipolar world and not allow anybody to come as a dominant power or a hegemonic power.

Co-Chairman's Concluding Remarks

Ambassador Gleb Ivanshentsov

I thank you all for very interesting and substantive discussions. I join Ambassador Mansingh in thanking you all and I think we have rightly deserved our lunch.

SESSION – II

PIVOT TO THE INDO-PACIFIC: TOWARDS GREATER STABILITY OR GREAT POWER RIVALRIES

Chairman	Vice Admiral Arun Kumar Singh, PVSM, AVSM, NM (Retd)
First Paper	Rear Admiral Sumihiko Kawamura (Retd)
Second Paper	Lt Gen Wallace Chip Gregson, Jr (Retd)
Third Paper	Rear Admiral Sudarshan Shrikhande
Discussion	
Concluding Remarks	Vice Admiral Arun Kumar Singh, PVSM, AVSM, NM (Retd)

Session – II

Chairman's Opening Remarks

Vice Admiral Arun Kumar Singh, PVSM, AVSM, NM (Retd)

Thank you and good afternoon ladies and gentlemen. The subject as you know is 'Pivot to Indo-Pacific – Towards Greater Stability or Great Power Rivalries'. I will just take a couple of minutes. History tends to repeat itself and there is rise and fall of civilisations. Lot of nations who ensured that China became a great power by trading with it includes United States, Japan, Australia, South Korea etc. They are all now feeling the heat. When we talk about US pivot to Asia, the Chinese have their own counter pivot to Asia. To take on this very very challenging subject, I would like our first speaker Rear Admiral Sumihiko Kawamura to kindly present his views.

Session – II

First Paper

Rear Admiral Sumihiko Kawamura (Retd)

Introductory Observation

China's fast growing economy and rapidly increased military capabilities undoubtedly will give it greater influence in the region even as the US 'pivot' or 'rebalance' towards the Asia-Pacific. A major source of growing tension in the region is China's excessive maritime claims and aggressive behaviour in its relationships with neighbouring countries.

US's rebalance will lead to 60 per cent of US Navy's assets deployed to the Asia-Pacific by 2020. Many countries in the region are looking to work closely with the United States in response to the rebalance. In reality, approximately 2,500 US Marines will deploy to Darwin in northern Australia; the Philippines will host more US troops on a rotating basis; Singapore will accept four US Littoral Combat Ships (LCS) for home-porting while Indonesia is seeking to procure a large amount of equipment and planning to conduct joint exercises with the United States. These are in addition to US's further strengthening of its defence ties with its long time allies in the region: Japan and RoK.

US's rebalance to the Asia-Pacific is viewed in China as a policy of containment and Beijing has criticized it severely. For the foreseeable future, the US-China relations will continue to go back and forth between cooperation and confrontation. As for US-China rivalries, the potential exists for the US-China rivalry to become more adversarial in the military-security arena. When considering the changing global environment, rivalry seems inevitable due to lack of common external enemy: ideological differences; and the gap between the two countries is becoming narrower.

More importantly, in accordance with its national strategic imperative, China is trying to play a zero-sum game in the South China Sea (SCS) to make the sea a sanctuary for its ballistic missile submarines' (SSBN) deployment in order to obtain credible nuclear deterrence capability. The United States is certain to prevent China from obtaining a credible second strike capability and Japan cannot be allowed to remain a bystander in this regard.

Now is the time to attach more importance to 'deterrence' rather than to 'negotiation' and the US-Japan alliance should take the lead to formulate a tacit cooperation scheme on a coalition among like-minded countries. Although conflict in the Asia-Pacific is undesirable and unlikely, the situation in the SCS remains fluid, and with the status of Taiwan still unresolved, a strategy is needed. Fortunately, much of the US strategy in the Asia-Pacific is based on classic conventional deterrence.

A primary strategic goal is to check China's ambition to control almost the entire area of the Indo-Pacific. Every country which shares the interests in the Indo-Pacific will be welcome to join the scheme assuming roles and missions concomitant to its geographical location, national power, military capabilities, etc. It is imperative that the US-Japan alliance devote the time, attention and resources necessary to forge an effective partnership with allies and like-minded countries to convert US rebalance from vision to reality.

Even though the US-China rivalry will fluctuate between "cooperation" and "confrontation" depending on China's response, so far as the US-Japan alliance pursues the above goal, it is highly likely that the rebalance will bring about the greater stability in the Indo-Pacific.

Security Situation in the Indo-Pacific

The South China Sea

The risk of conflict in the SCS is increasing. In the 1990s, access to the undersea oil and gas reserves as well as fishing and ocean resources began to complicate various countries' claims.

As world energy demand has increased, claimants have devised plans to exploit the undersea energy reserves with disputes continuing, particularly between China and the neighbouring countries; China has a voracious appetite for the undersea energy resource.

A major source of growing tension in the SCS is China's territorial and maritime claims of sovereignty over much of the entire sea (i.e. the nine-dashed line). China's interests bear a strong territorial character, which flows from its revisionist policy and national objective of 'territorial consolidation.'

In the SCS, China is in conflict with such ASEAN countries as the Philippines and Vietnam regarding sovereignty over the Spratly Islands and other islands and reefs. China asserts a claim of exclusive sovereignty over not only the Spratly Islands but nearly all of the SCS, yet it has not brought the international community around to its point of view.

For over a decade, the ASEAN countries have been trying to secure agreement from China on the establishment of rules of conduct to prevent hostilities in the SCS yet, with its overwhelming military and economic power, China has refused to hold such a meeting until recently. It is regrettable that even when China finally did come to the negotiating table, it proposed discussing other issues instead and would not go into a detailed discussion on a SCS code of conduct.

In the SCS, with no code of conduct for concerned countries, the crisis is only deepening. China continues to pursue an aggressive maritime expansion in the SCS and in the East China Sea (ECS) while invoking nationalism at home to deflect criticism of the dictatorship by the Chinese Communist Party.

China is certain to have strategic intention to make the SCS a sanctuary for its SSBNs in order to obtain credible sea-based nuclear retaliation capability.

At present, the issue has gone beyond territorial claims and access to energy resources; the SCS has become a focal area for the US-China rivalry in the Indo-Pacific. Since the USNS Impeccable incident in March 2009, the SCS has become linked with wider strategic issues with regard to China's naval strategy and US forward presence in the region.

The East China Sea

In the ECS, China has raised the stakes by sending a steady stream of non-naval patrol ships, surveillance aircraft, and fighter aircraft into a contentious area. The ongoing tension over the Senkaku islands dispute escalated further following claims that Chinese warships' fire control radars near the islands "locked on" to a Japanese helicopter and destroyer in separate incidents in January.

A Chinese Foreign Ministry Official clarified on 26 April 2013 that the Senkaku Islands are part of China's core interest concerning its territorial sovereignty.

The purchase of three of the Senkaku Islands by the Japanese Government in September 2012 appeared to China as a further attempt by Japan to strengthen its control of these islands, infuriating Beijing even more.

China has lately been more vocal in asserting its maritime territorial claims along its entire maritime periphery in the SCS and ECS provoking the neighbouring countries into contention by waging Military Operations Other Than War (MOOTW), making full use of non-military assets such as patrol ships and surveillance aircraft.

The Indian Ocean

The maritime powers in the Indian Ocean are defining their strategic interests as they interact with each other.

While the United States was bogged down in Iraq and Afghanistan, China obtained beachheads to expand its influence in the Indian Ocean region such as 'the String of Pearls' with its friends: Pakistan, Myanmar, and Sri Lanka.

Over the long-term, China's emergence as regional power in the Indian Ocean, will have the potential to affect the economy and security of India, the United States and other maritime countries in many ways.

The areas of maritime interests of India and China broadly overlap. Therefore, there are possibilities of conflict between India and China in the future, especially if China pursues development of its own capabilities both in power projection and sea-denial in addition to the infrastructure to support them in accordance with its Indian Ocean strategy.

In reality, attack submarines from the Chinese navy are becoming increasingly active in the Indian Ocean region, posing a grave threat to India's interests there. A report from the Ministry of Defence of India said in April 2013 that at least 22 contacts, very likely from the Chinese submarines, had been made in the Indian Ocean region in 2012 alone.

In the Indo-Pacific, it is certain that the United States, China and India need to work together to advance common economic and security interests. However, both the United States and India share the common goal of not wanting an Indo-Pacific that is dominated by China. But at the same time, India is not likely to become a traditional ally of the United States eager to balance or counter China's efforts.

The shared objective for the United States and India is how to build a stable balance of power in the Indian Ocean region, and there is a large area for the United States and India to collaborate.

The Goal of China's Strategy in the Indo-Pacific

While China is conducting various maritime activities in the SCS and ESC such as operations to comply with the imperatives for natural resources and to facilitate SLOC security, the ultimate goal of China's strategy is to obtain credible nuclear retaliation capability in the SCS and to become a military super power, a rival competitor of the United States.

If China succeeds to make the SCS a sanctuary for SSBN deployments, it would provide China with an opportunity to obtain credible sea-based nuclear deterrence capability and upstage the current US nuclear superiority.

Possessing a credible sea-based nuclear deterrent capability is a priority for China's military strategy and the following constitute the rationale of China's bastion strategy in the SCS:-

(a) In the adjacent waters around China, only the SCS provides waters deep enough to ensure the safe deployment of SSBNs.

(b) China has constructed a large naval base including an underground submarine bunker in Sanya, Hainan Island in the SCS.

(c) China has built three Type-94, Jin-class SSBNs equipped with 12 missile tubes for JL-2 submarine-launched ballistic missiles (SLBM) with estimated range of 8,000 Km and two of which were confirmed to have been moored alongside a pier in Sanya. Some estimates that these SSBNs will be fully operational in 2014.

(d) The PLA Navy's first aircraft carrier, the Liaoning and its successors are highly likely to be deployed in the SCS, as it seems to be unable to conduct genuine carrier operations in the open ocean. However, SSBN protection operations under the air cover provided by land-based aircraft will be the only imaginable mission for the aircraft carrier.

(e) China continues the development to extend combat range to cover the Continental United States (CONUS).

(f) China is developing A2/AD capabilities to protect the SCS and ECS.

During the Cold War, the Soviet Union (USSR) turned to its SSBN force as insurance against US capabilities to destroy Soviet land-based ICBMs. The need to secure its SSBN force from attack by US anti-submarine forces meant that Soviet SSBNs had to be deployed in home waters with SLBMs of sufficient range to strike CONUS. In addition to the Barents Sea, the USSR gave priority to making the Sea of Okhotsk a safe haven for the Delta-class SSBNs by fortifying the Defence of the Kuril Islands and reinforcing the Pacific Fleet at Vladivostok. Ultimately, the Soviet Pacific Fleet deployed more than 100 submarines together with 140 surface combatants including two Kiev-class V/STOL aircraft carriers, to protect its SSBN force in the Sea of Okhotsk.

Similarly, China needs to protect its SSBNs in the SCS and modify its maritime strategy. With the commissioning of the Jin-class SSBN, protection of SSBNs is likely to become another primary mission of the PLA Navy. This mission will require China to keep the

SCS off-limits, preventing attacks from adversary ASW forces, and to silence other claimants in the SCS. According the Jane's Fighting Ships 2012-2013, a total of six Jin-class submarines is expected, with the sixth unit projected to be commissioned in 2016.

It is certain that China will be able to obtain credible nuclear retaliation capabilities if it succeeds in making the SCS a sanctuary for its SSBNs and in extending SLBM range slightly.

The US Response in the Indo-Pacific

The rivalry in the SCS became more intense in 2010 following Secretary of Defence Robert Gates' statement in Singapore in June 2010 and Secretary of State Hillary Clinton's reaffirmation of the US policy of returning to the region after a long period of absence at the ASEAN Regional Forum (ARF) in Hanoi in July 2010. These statements opened a new dimension in regional security dynamics.

In his remarks to the Australian Parliament in November 2011, President Barack Obama asserted the importance of America's rebalance to the Asia-Pacific, stating that as a Pacific nation, the United States will play a long-term role in shaping this region and its future by upholding core principles and in close partnership with its allies and friends."

The Obama administration stopped calling its efforts to focus on Asia the "pivot" which implies turning USA's back on other crucial parts of the world and introduced the term "rebalance" instead. Thereby the Obama administration declared its intension to shift the US focus to the Asia-Pacific region.

The rebalance is driven by a desire to guarantee US allies, friends, and other countries in the region that the United States has neither been exhausted after a decade of war nor has it been weakened by economic and political problems at home and that it is not going to stay away from Asia-Pacific affairs.

The rebalance rests on five pillars: strengthened and modernised security alliances across the region; deeper partnership with emerging powers; deeper engagement in global and regional institutions to promote regional cooperation; the peaceful resolution of disputes, and adherence to human rights, and international law; stable and constructive relationship with China; and advancing the region's economic architecture.

So far as we see the rhetoric of rebalance, it is not a strategy to contain China. However, China remains skeptical, even though Beijing has been eased to some extent by US's attempt to give reassurance on its intentions and its emphasis on the diplomatic dimension rather than military one of the newly adopted policy.

There should be no doubt that implementation of the new policy will impact China. But the degree to which it targets China depends on Chinese behaviour. If China chooses to act as revisionist agenda that aggressively challenging the norms, rules and institutions of global order, the United States along with like-minded countries, is certain to respond accordingly.

The overarching US national policy objectives of the rebalance are as follows:-

(a) Maintain peace, stability, the free flow of commerce, and US influence in the Asia-Pacific region.

(b) Maintain regional access and the ability to operate freely.

(c) Build a healthy, transparent, and sustainable US-China Defence relationship that also supports a broader US-China relationship.

As for the ways at the national level, the five pillars of rebalance strategy have been identified are as follows:-

(a) Strengthening alliances.

(b) Deepening partnerships.

(c) Empowering regional institutions.

(d) Building a stable, productive, and constructive relationship with China.

(e) Helping to build a regional economic architecture that can sustain shared prosperity.

The Nature of US-China Rivalry

The US and Chinese conflicting interpretations on "freedom of navigation" have resulted in several incidents in the EEZs of the SCS and ECS. China has expressed concern over the US's increasing engagement in the SCS, adding that it opposes the internationalisation of the issue. China holds that the SCS issues are disputes over sovereign territory and maritime rights between relevant countries, and are not issues between China and ASEAN as a whole, nor are they regional or international matters.

China's opposition to the "internationalisation" of the SCS issue is equivalent to an attempt to de-internationalisation of an international sea. If the SCS is de-internationalised, China can bring its strength to bear on Southeast Asian countries and impose its own rules, rather than rules promulgated by international law. Neither compromises nor concessions from China over maritime rights and territorial sovereignty in the SCS are likely, as Beijing's primary aim to control the entire waters of the SCS deriving from China's national strategic objective, not only from its imperatives for natural resources.

On the other hand, much of the US strategy in the Asia-Pacific is based on classic conventional deterrence, and American diplomats have a clear strategy of wishing to engage China and develop close ties to lessen tensions. However, situations in the SCS and ECS remain fluid; the status of Taiwan remains unresolved even as China military grows ever more capable of forcing the issue. In reality, the US military has already moved critical nuclear attack submarines, Aegis missile platforms, and naval surface combatants to bases in Guam and Japan. And there is widespread talk of the implementation of "Air Sea Battle Concept," which is aimed at defeating an opponent's anti-access weaponry.

Since the summit meeting between US President Barack Obama and Chinese President Xi Jinping in June, once heightened the tense US-China rivalry has shown signs of softening, following a series of high-level military visit and the invitation to China to participate in the biennial Rim of the Pacific Exercise (RIMPAC) in 2014. However, the potential still exists for the US-China relationship to become much more adversarial, in the military- security arena. When considering the roots of rivalry between the two countries and changing global environment, the tension seems inevitable.

Firstly, the United States and China lack a common enemy. Even though there are global and regional issues such as greenhouse gas emission control, the proliferation of weapons of mass destruction, terrorism and piracy, these issues are not enough to ensure close security cooperation between the two countries. They do not share an imminent common threat of a country or a group of countries.

Secondly, both countries have sharp ideological differences. Even though China has adopted a market-oriented economy, it is still a country under a Communist Party's dictatorship. Disparity is about value systems, more than about confrontation between liberal democracy and authoritarianism. These value systems include the concept of human rights, religious freedom, freedom of speech, and rule of law.

Thirdly, with the rapid development of China, the gap between the two countries is becoming smaller, and it cannot be denied that there is psychological tension between an established but presumably declining power on one side and rising power on the other.

China is now the second-largest economy in the world, and many believe it will surpass the United States before 2030. The United States and China are not likely to enter into an actual conflict; however, it is difficult to imagine that both countries will agree to collaborate for shared leadership in the Indo-Pacific. It is easier to imagine a continued contest for a favourable position. Thus, the risk of conflict resulting from continued confrontation is still high for the two countries and roots of rivalry which could result in confrontation are very solid. For the foreseeable future, the US-China relations will continue to go back and forth between cooperation and confrontation.

Conclusion

As a result of the rebalance, the diplomatic rivalry has begun to divide the Indo-Pacific region into two blocs: one is a maritime nations' group composed primarily of liberal democracies, including India, Japan, Australia, RoK, Philippines and Taiwan; the other is a continental nations' group of relatively poor, authoritarian countries adjacent to China's periphery, including North Korea, Laos, Cambodia and Pakistan.

It is natural that China has shown little interest in diplomatic settlement and won't rule out the use of force to claim and control the SCS and ECS. The key which could change China's calculations might be the deterrence derived from the improved security ties between the United States and other maritime nations. If the US-Japan alliance succeeds to establish a regional cooperation scheme in the form of a "non-alliance" maritime security coalition, China could be deterred.

Japanese Prime Minister Shinzo Abe, since he took office in December 2012, has intensively visited ASEAN countries and has presented his plan of providing ten patrol ships to the Philippines.

For both the United States and Japan, which face the expanding presence of China in the Indo-Pacific, the significance of cooperating with ASEAN member countries in addition to India by taking concerted actions with them is not limited to the SCS. It will help their efforts to check China from expanding its maritime activities elsewhere as well.

The maritime nations need to start discussions on how to deter Chinese aggression. As for such discussions, the United States has differences with several of the countries in Southeast Asia regarding where and what kind of military operations can be done in international waters, including EEZ.

The countries' logical support of the US Navy presence does not currently extend to endorsing naval surveillance and other operations necessary to carry out its missions. This should be an important area of negotiations among the United States and its allies, partners and friends.

Session – II

Second Paper

Lt Gen Wallace "Chip" Gregson, Jr (Retd)

The Changing Geo-Strategic Landscape - Pivot, Policy, and Strategy Rethinking Security Planning Models

The "Baby Boomer" generation, author included, of America grew up listening to living memory of the Depression, and of the wars in Europe and the Pacific. It watched veterans recalled to active duty in someplace called Korea. It was a "police action", a limited war, a new thing in the wake of the largest total war in history. Before it was over the fought Chinese forces, recent victors in China's long civil war. The Cold War – another new phenomenon - emerged, an existential struggle thankfully waged without direct superpower combat. I Grade schools practiced diving under desks for protection from fallout. Anti-aircraft missile sites appeared around industrial cities and government locations. The US made allies of recent enemies, and recent allies became enemies. The Marshall and other foreign aid flowed to support freedom and democracy. NSC 68 gave national security structure to wage the Cold War. Most of US was assigned to math, science, or engineering curricula following the Soviet Sputnik launch in 1957. We were told that we were behind, and had to catch up. Many of us were called to "bear any burden, pay any price" in a place called Vietnam. That national security structure endures still, with a few additions – no deletions - to accommodate the challenge made manifest on 11 September 2001.

Cold War exigencies drove governmental Organisation, military planning and procurement, foreign policy, industrial policy, school curricula, and even the Interstate Highway System. The reality of nuclear weapons limited direct US-USSR combat action, creating various "hot" campaigns of proxy wars under that umbrella. The world divided into the "Communist Bloc", the "Free World", and the "Non-Aligned". It was a pretty ugly era of competing throw-weights, fallout shelters and worries over strontium 90 in milk from nuclear tests. But it was conceptually simple. Alliances and blocs competed, we had sides, we had structure, and we had a central organizing principle. The Organisation of the world was clear, our policy and strategy had a clear focus, and our military-industrial complex had a model shaping our planning and operations. Our government enjoyed a compelling reason for taxing the American public, for compulsory military service, and for the many hot campaigns, large and small, over 70 in all, within the otherwise "Cold" War.

Then suddenly, surprisingly, the reason for all this was gone. Our enemy left the field. But not as a result of a clash of arms or a formal surrender ceremony. It just ceased to exist, collapsing from the inside from economic and ideological exhaustion. The preoccupation and the reason for existence of our national security establishment – government, military, science, education and civilian industry – went away. Incredibly, it was not predicted. We were so focused on the threat that we missed the obvious. It's hard to find an apt historical example. Even the fall of Rome was more obvious and lengthy.

Perhaps the simplest description of the impact of the Soviet collapse on our security institutions is found in popular Pentagon lore. As the Soviet Union was collapsing, the Chairman of the Joint Chiefs of Staff summoned his Chairman's Study Group. This 4-person group was three colonels and a Navy captain, chosen carefully by each service chief. The Chairman had a simple question: "What do we do now that we've lost our best enemy?"

In many ways we are still looking for a new "best enemy". Life was much simpler for our bureaucratic functions when we had a single, well-defined villain, right out of central casting. The villain is gone. China is most definitely not the new answer.

Enduring Principles and the Pivot

With the demise of the Soviet Union, the US should be returning to the cardinal principles of traditional strategy and policy. The US, despite our changing emphasis from time to time, has been remarkably consistent in a few cardinal principles of policy and strategy since at least the presidency of Teddy Roosevelt – support of democracy and the pursuit of democratic peace. We've always believed that democratic societies support peaceful resolution of disputes, human rights, contract law, economic development, free trade and commerce better than any other government model.

The Asia-Pacific region is now our stated focus. This region poses greater potential for incredible progress and economic success alongside instability and tension than others. In our globalized and interconnected world, any crisis or confrontation here affects peace, stability, security and prosperity everywhere.

Secretary Clinton provided the most enduring description of our emerging policy in Asia and the Pacific. She said, we stand at a "pivot point" as we prepare to withdraw from Iraq and Afghanistan, that we have to be smart and systematic about where we invest our time and energy, and that "One of the most important tasks of American statecraft over the next decade will therefore be to lock in a substantially increased diplomatic, economic and strategic investment and otherwise in the Asia-Pacific region."

"Asia and the Pacific", the object of our rebalancing and realignment, stretches from the Indian sub-continent to the western shores of the Americas, north and south. It spans two oceans that are increasingly linked by shipping, energy, trade, and strategy. It includes five US treaty allies. It includes sovereign US territory, one island nation in Covenant with the United States that is treated like a territory, and three island nations in Compacts of Free Association with the US. It includes the world's most populous country, and its future most populous country. The world's largest and second largest Muslim populations within single national boundaries are in this region. It's home to three maritime straits – the Malacca, the Sunda, and the Lombok - that permit the easy passage of well over 1100 fully laden supertankers per year, most passing on into the South China Sea bringing energy to China, Japan, the Republic of Korea, Taiwan, and other countries.

This body of water is bounded by China, Vietnam, the Philippines,

Brunei, Malaysia, Indonesia, Taiwan, and Singapore. Many nations have competing claims to various islands and reefs in the South China Sea, and thus competing claims to fishing grounds, sea-bed resources, and exclusive economic zones. Fifty percent of the world's seaborne commercial tonnage and one-third of the world's value in trade traverse this sea.

Traditional international law, as favoured by the United States, calls for freedom of navigation and peaceful settlement of disputes. This is being increasingly challenged by China's claim of historical rights to the entire South and East China seas.

China

In the early 15th Century China was the world's maritime superpower. Admiral Zheng He, a Chinese Muslim Eunuch Conscript sailed the ocean sea. His fleet was bigger than Spain's famous armada, still 150 years or more in the future. He sailed across all of Asia, bringing treasure, tribute, and foreign envoys back to the Middle Kingdom. Never defeated in battle, the fleet was brought low by imperial edict in 1433, as China faced hostilities on its land borders.

China is again pulled in two divergent directions by continental and maritime interests. Fourteen land powers share terrestrial frontiers with China while six maritime countries together enclose the entire Chinese coastline. Of these twenty neighbouring states, six rank among the world's top ten in population, eight rank among the top twenty-five in military forces, and four possess nuclear weapons.

China settled twelve of fourteen land border disputes. China no longer has any natural enemies on her borders, but neither does she have any natural friends. The closest "friends" might be North Korea and Pakistan. China does not have any natural seafaring partners among the six nations on her seaward frontier.

Beginning in 2009 and accelerating in 2010 and 2011, China began exerting ever more pressure on the East and South China Seas with expanding territorial claims and action, from encroaching fishing vessels to seabed drilling rights. These seas bathe the home of China's industry, economy, and wealth. The GDP per capita in the greater coastal region area is seven to ten times higher than it is inland. In no other place in the world do the critical interests of so many states overlap. China would accrue immense strategic benefits if these became the equivalent of inland seas. The offshore states would face correspondingly great disadvantages. This region must be very carefully managed to ensure continued peace and tranquility.

Regional Trends

The Asia and Pacific region as a whole has many built-in stresses that can cause conflict. Some of the more dominant, or powerful, include demographics, energy, food and agricultural, and fresh water.

The world will add nearly 60 million people per year, reaching over eight billion by the 2030s. Most growth will be in developing countries. The United States, alone among developed countries, is expected to add 50 million people. Europe, Japan, Russia, and Korea will join those in absolute population decline.

China will add some 170 million, but the population will be aging, and predominantly male. India, in contrast, will add 320 million people, becoming the world's most populous nation before 2030.

India will continue to grow, risking tension between the rich and the poor, as well as among Hindus, Muslims, and Buddhists. The Maoists in much of eastern India are India's most important security challenge, according to the Indians themselves.

Rapid development in China, India, and other countries creates a relentless drive to assure adequate and secure supplies of fuel to sustain growth, maintain satisfaction, and prevent internal strife and chaos.

Every fresh water system on the East, Southeast, and South Asian littoral is under heavy pressure from pollution. The search for affordable energy invites upstream countries to build hydroelectric dams on rivers coming out of their mountains. Ungoverned, this can cause devastation to downstream nations.

Nuclear issues, both weapons and power generation, are a reality in Asia. The United States, Russia, and China essentially balance and deter one another. But another relationship is that among China, India and Pakistan.

China keeps a careful eye on India's nuclear arsenal. Meanwhile, Pakistan is rapidly building its arsenal. If India increases its arsenal, this puts pressure on China to react. Increasing China's arsenal affects the US-China-Russia balance.

North Korea's nuclear weapons program affects our allies and friends. Many voices call for independent nuclear capabilities. US presence and strong involvement is essential to our guarantees of extended deterrence to prevent an arms race.

Terror networks and their sponsors are already present in Asia. They gain support from financial flows, both formal and illicit. The North Korean leadership will sell anything to those with cash. They are widely suspected to be in league with Iran's nuclear ambitions.

Defence Strategy Development

Into this threatening mix we add the rise of China. Historically, emergence of a rising power within a system of established powers threatens peace and stability. Most often this leads to an unhappy ending. China is not the Soviet Union. "Containment" is out of the question. It has a robust economy linked to the US, our allies and friends, and the rest of the world. Not one of our allies and friends wants us to pick a fight with China, but they do want us to help protect their interests. Our challenge today is much more varied and complex than before. Conversely, we need clarity in our intentions, our policy, and our strategy. We must be especially clear, and public, about our military strategy, as a nation and ally if we are to contribute to deterrence and ensure the ability to prevail if necessary while not adding to the inherent tension.

The Center for Strategic and International Studies recently completed a critical assessment of our Pacific posture for Congress. That study made clear the prime goal of regional peace and security and the role of our force presence. They concluded, in part:

"There are clear connections between shaping actions and contingency preparation. Given rapid advances in Chinese military capabilities, the consequences of conflict with that nation are almost unthinkable and should be avoided to the greatest extent possible, consistent with US interests. It is therefore critical to achieve the right combination of assurance and dissuasion and to maintain a favourable peace before conflict occurs. At the same time, the ability of the United States to work with allies and partners to achieve those peaceful ends will depend on the perceptions, both of allies and partners of China, of the US ability to prevail in the event of conflict. US force posture must demonstrate a readiness and a capacity to fight and win, even under more challenging circumstances associated with A2AD and other threats to US military operations in the Western Pacific. Demonstrating such capacity is not automatic; one way to undercut dramatically the regional confidence in the US commitment and the American ability to shape decisions and preserve peace would be to adopt a posture that pulled back from the Western Pacific and focused only on the survivability of US forces and reductions in annual costs of forward presence. Forward presence and engagement are not simply helpful to shaping the environment and setting the stage for effective responses to contingencies – they are indispensable for minimizing the likelihood of larger conflicts."[1]

Strategies, properly done, have a discipline. Professor Eliot Cohen insists that proper strategies include critical assumptions, ends-ways-means coherence, priorities, sequencing, and a theory of victory. Another distinguished scholar, Colin Gray, advises that strategies must be cognizant of additional factors: intellect, morality, culture, geography, and technology.

Ends-ways-means coherence is especially necessary in an era of constrained security resources. Strategy must support deterrence and provide assurance of prevailing in the event of conflict. The history of conflict between nuclear armed powers, so far, shows both sides avoiding escalation and direct attack. Ensuring the security of our allies' territory and interests and constraining escalation must be our most important end. American and allied morality and culture support a defensive strategy. The relevant geography tied to our interests includes vast archipelagos of thousands of offshore islands from north to south. Technological trends include rapidly expanding surveillance and targeting capabilities, guided weapons increasingly accurate at distance, sophisticated communications, and emerging

---

1 US Force Posture Strategy in the Asia Pacific Region: An Independent Assessment. Center for Strategic and International Studies, 10 July 2012 pages 17-18.

space and cyberspace capabilities. We may be entering an era when the day's technology favours the Defence. In this respect, 2013 looks like 1913. We need to avoid that century's mistakes.

Our strategy must be declared and developed with our allies, principally Japan as owner of the archipelago defining the East China Sea and the northern half of the First Island Chain. This is necessary to reassure allies and friends of our defensive intentions and to counter persistent characterization of our intentions as aggressive attack. Our joint command element in Japan must be given operational capability and the authority to develop the alliance strategy's details and drive the bi-lateral training necessary for implementation. Nesting such a strategy within our overall government policies supporting peace, security, stability and prosperity for all will enhance cooperation and deterrence while providing assurance and dissuasion.

Session – II

Third Paper

Rear Admiral Sudarshan Shrikhande, IN

"Fear, Honour & Interest": The Wake And The Bow Wave of The Dynamics of The Indo-Pacific

Although said in the 4th century BCE, Thucydides rings eternally true in stating, through the voices of the Athenian delegates, their refusal "to give it (i.e. their empire) up under the pressure of three of the strongest motives, fear, honour and interest." [1]

In this paper, the writer would like to try and look into the wake of the history of the region we now choose to call the Indo-Pacific, and see how these Thucydidian drivers, Fear, Honour and Interest influenced war, conquest, empires and even uneasy peace over more than two centuries. These three pressures, not surprisingly, would also continue to be essential components of conflict, confrontation, compromise, consolidation and cooperation in the decades ahead. That is the bow-wave we will try and look at. It is useful and important that we examine the past for similarities as well as differences, to better understand the rippled surface of the Indo-Pacific region.

It is less important to dissect the hyphenated geography or the origin of the term Indo-Pacific or even of its first use than to look at what has happened in this region in times past. One could argue that nations, and often their navies, have looked at these two oceans and the lands that reside or about them in a more unitary fashion for at least two centuries. Arguably, medieval China also did that. The weakness of the argument in over-interpreting Zheng He's voyages is not because they were not intrepid but because they did not contribute

---

1   Robert Strassler, ed; "The Landmark Thycydides:A Comprehensive Guide to the Peloponnesian War;"1.76, p 43.

to any discernible and sustained strategic dividend for China either through trade or planting of the flag in distant lands.[2] However, the voyages of European navigators like Magellan and Cook, the intimate and intricate marriage between their trade and their flags shaped, and re-shaped the strategic geography of the region. Not surprisingly, the "rationale" for conquest, conflict, compromise or co-operation echoed and re-echoed through the 19th and 20th centuries. The 21st century is also likely to hear these refrains. It may be important, therefore to look into the wake and think about what today's bow wave may bring to the surface. What fears, honour or interests would under- write tomorrow's placidity or tomorrow's turbulence?

Let us look back to the final decades of the 19th and the early years of the 20th century. What was happening in the Indo- Pacific?

(a) Hawaii was effectively annexed by the US a few years before formalisation in 1898. Interestingly, two Japanese ships made a tentative show of force in 1897 by entering Honolulu. Less than forty years had passed since Commodore Perry's squadron had made its presence felt in Japanese waters. These were unlike the friendly visits that JMSDF ships make today for the US- hosted RIMPAC Exercises! And, by the way, for the first time Indian Navy units are also scheduled to participate in the next RIMPAC. [3]

(b) The Imperial Japanese Navy (IJN) was riding the crest of an impressive victory in the first Sino- Japanese War of 1894-95.[4]

(c) The stage was set for a clash between the Russian and the Japanese empires. Russia was expanding eastwards to acquire warm water ports in the Pacific. The Tsar was perhaps pivoting

---

2 q.v. Malik, Ashok. "Stories that Await a Storyteller." The Asian Age, 22 Sep 2013, op ed. Like, Zheng He's revival, the author recommends that India should look carefully at the maritime exploits of the Cholas of Southern India and their use of the naval instrument in their kingdom's interest.

3 Joint US–India Statement 27 Sep 2013; Embassy of India, Wash DC website.

4 The rise of the IJN in a relatively short period from infancy to victory at Tsushima is a fascinating and important story. This writer has studied the way in which the IJN became an instrument for Japan; how it admirably indigenised itself in a manner that can be seen in the PLA Navy. IJN's training, tactics, thinking hold important lessons for Navies for do's as well as don'ts! This includes the perils of sometimes advocating-- and often not objecting to-- faulty strategic thinking.

to the Pacific. (of course, no one used the word then! It is no surprise that the Mackinderian term used by Americans in 2010, changed into the less irascible "rebalancing" a little later.) We must remember that the 1858 Treaty of Aigun settled the border with China on terms more favourable for the Russians than had happened after the Nerchinsk Treaty of 1689. The 1858 treaty enabled Russia to spread towards Vladivostok, a name that literally means "Ruler of the East". It may not be wrong to say that the reasons for the 1969 clashes between communist Russia and China over the Amur- Ussuri region had their origins centuries before that. Honour, remains an emotive or at times a convenient driver even as regimes change. For example, Chinese thoughts on honour (core interests) and their role in international relations changed with the fall of Stalin; with the American withdrawal and impending defeat in Vietnam; or, in current times, with more money, and more muscle and a growing assertiveness. Honour is a long-lasting sentiment that can be inflamed or starved of oxygen depending on the value of interests or the degree of fear on one or multiple sides. It may also be useful to remember that these were times in which British strategists in London or in colonial Calcutta thought that Russia was looking at access to ports not only in the Far East, but into the Indian Ocean as well. In the closing and opening decades of the 19th- 20th centuries the "Great Game" had many teams, playing by different rules. Is something similar happening in the opening decades of this century?

(d) The build-up of military power in Japan was not really a secret. Yet, prejudiced European lenses were not in short supply. "The Japanese Army is an army of infants...it will take one hundred years for (them) to have the moral foundations of the weakest army in Europe," said a Russian attaché in Japan.[5] "Yellow Peril" was a term coined in Wilhelmine Germany but used all over the West.

(e) For a host of reasons, the US was looking to break up the

---

5 Wolff, David. Et al., *The Russo- Japanese War in Global Perspective* (Leiden- Boston, Brill, 2007), p. 13.

Spanish empire in two oceans. It prepared to fight Spain over Cuba in the Atlantic and for Philippines in the Pacific. The Spanish- American war of 1898 made the US an imperial player in the Pacific. Unlike today, it did not see the need for a Trans- Pacific Partnership at the dawn of the 20th century! In 1890, the year that Alfred Thayer Mahan published his first book and claimed fame, the US had begun shaping the environment to build a canal through the Isthmus of Panama. Work began in May 1904. At around the same time, the IJN was putting in place its final plans to land troops on the Liaodong peninsula, decimate the Tsarist Pacific fleet and blockade Port Arthur.

The "Great Game" referred to had a forward player in India by the name of George Curzon, the Viceroy and the backs and half-backs were in the "India Office" in London with some forwards in Egypt, Cairo, Kabul and elsewhere in the Middle East.[6] Curzon stayed in the game for several years thereafter to see imperial Russia disappear; the Red Army fight a civil war in which several powers were involved to restore the "ancient regime". In the event, Vladivostok was a point of ingress for many nations, America included.

Today, on the very large Indo- Pacific stage the actors and some backdrops may have changed; the script is more reflective of today's political terminology; smaller- actors are numerous with occasionally important lines to deliver; and the big stars seem to be ageing or trying hard to be part of the larger cast. Also, in earlier times, the word imperial was not considered embarrassing by many actors, much as the term democracy is in vogue today. (Even North Korea has a D in DPRK!)

Let us turn once again to Japan. Several matters of contemporary interest emerge in looking at the Japan of those decades. In 1901, Australian Prime Minister, Alfred Deakin introduced the so-called White Australia policy with a political incorrectness-and twisted candour- that would be very difficult in our times:

---

6 A very interesting chapter by John Gooch expands the Great Game into and after the First World War. See Ch 8, *"Building Buffers and Filling Vacuums: Great Britain and the Middle East, 1914- 1922"* in the book, *The Making of Peace: Rulers, States, and the Aftermath of War.* Ed. Murray, Lacey; Cambridge Univ Press, 2009.

"It is not the bad qualities, but the good qualities of these alien races (ie the Japanese and the Chinese) that make them dangerous to us. It is their inexhaustible energy, their power of applying themselves to new tasks, their endurance and low standard of living that make them such competitors."[7]

We had a modernising Japan, as well as a China emerging from the depredations of two Opium Wars, the Boxer Rebellion, foreign troops, legations and the burden of reparations and constraining treaties. They were both very discontent with immigration restrictions, not only in Australia, but in the Americas as well. Contrast this with the much more polite language used today in imposing visa restrictions, whatever be the underlying economic and political motivations. During the Paris Conference of 1919, Japan had proposed a racial equality clause in the covenant of the League of Nations. PM Billy Hughes of Australia opposed it. Australia believed that Japan, with a powerful navy, a large army and already demonstrated presence in Korea, Manchuria and in some ex-German colonial possessions in the South Pacific, was now virtually a geographic neighbour. (That the IJN and the Royal Australian Navy operated in concert throughout the First World War became immaterial.) The failure of the clause did not go down well in Japan and contributed to intensification of nationalism, and a desire to set the agenda, backed by hard power. That Koreans or Chinese did not feel the breeze of racial liberalism that Japan espoused in Paris was a matter of detail that Japan could afford to ignore in those times. In Paris, Baron Nobukai declared at a press conference:-

"We are not too proud to fight but are too proud to accept a place of admitted inferiority in dealing with one or more of the associated nations. We want nothing but simple justice."[8]

It is, therefore, worth noting that in our own times Japan needs immigrants for economic reasons, but thwarts them due to political compulsions.

Having won wars against the Chinese and the Russian Pacific

---

7 http://www.latrobe.edu.au/AHR/archive/issue/Jun-2001/schaffer.html.

8 Lauren, Paul Gordon. *Power and Prejudice: The Politics and Diplomacy of Racial Discrimination*. Waterview Press (1988).

fleet, Japan stirred the world as never before when it destroyed the Tsar's Baltic fleet in the Strait of Tsushima. Not only was this a decisive naval victory, it impacted in several ways. Although Japan was a British ally, the King's unhappy subjects in India and non-European races across Asia and Africa saw this as a game-changer. In the prologue to his book "From the Ruins of Empire: The Revolt Against the West and the Remaking of Asia", Pankaj Mishra's opening lines are worth recounting:-

"The contemporary world first began to assume its decisive shape over two days in May 1905. In what is now one of the busiest shipping lanes in the world, a small Japanese fleet annihilated much of the Russian navy. Described by the German Kaiser as the most important naval battle since Trafalgar, and by President Theodore Roosevelt as 'the greatest phenomenon the world has ever seen'… for the first time since the Middle Ages, a non-European country had vanquished a European power in a major war; and the news careened around the world that Western imperialists, and the invention of the telegraph, had closely knit together." [9]

Curzon, the viceroy in India, "feared that 'the reverberations of that victory have gone like a thunderclap through the whispering galleries of the East." In South Africa, an Indian lawyer, later known as the iconic Mahatma Gandhi, predicted 'so far and wide have the roots of Japanese victory spread that we cannot now visualise all the fruit it will put forth.' In a train from Dover to London, a young Indian, Jawaharlal Nehru had thought about his own role in 'Indian freedom and Asiatic freedom from the thraldom of Europe." Another future leader, Sun Yat-sen was in London when he heard the news and was exultant and later surprised at being congratulated by Arab workers along the Suez Canal who thought he was Japanese! [10] This "victory also startled Roosevelt who began to see Japan as a threat."[11] Reluctantly, but wisely, he accepted a secret request from Japan; the US brokered peace between the belligerents at Portsmouth. In a sense,

9 Mishra, ibid. p 1. (Allen Lane, 2012). For students of the "Indo- Pacific" this book is of value in offering a non- Western perspective on a world from Egypt to Japan as it went through change over more than a century.

10 Mishra, ibid. p. 1-2.

11 E.B. Potter. *Sea Power: A Naval History*. USNI Press, 1981, p. 193

the US had already played a role in support of Japan and against Britain via a $200 million loan from a rich American banker, Joseph Shiff. This loan had partially enabled Japan to arm herself in time for the war with Russia. (Today perhaps it is the wealth, measured in US dollars, and its sustained economic strength and influence that enable China to arm itself so impressively?) Having won the Nobel for Peace, Roosevelt sailed the Great White Fleet around the world in 1907. This did not go down well with the Japanese or the British, but everyone pretended to welcome the sailors. We must keep in mind that in the Russo-Japanese War, France, an ally of Russia, did not assist it against the Japanese. This is the quandary that smaller or weaker partners often face; there are no guarantees that a promise will be kept. Today, would the US automatically intervene militarily on behalf of Japan, South Korea or Taiwan in a skirmish or conflict with China? How does one nation sell the idea of its honour and interests to coalition partners or allies, enhance their fears and come off better through diplomacy or the big stick?

In those decades, the Royal Navy was quite active with a relatively small footprint in the Far East and Pacific. It had also proved its worth at the other end of the Indian Ocean in supporting the hard-pressed Army in the Boer War. In 1902, the Anglo-Japanese Alliance helped cement the maritime relationship. England needed an ally to keep the Russians in check in the Pacific. London and Tokyo had drawn closer over several decades after their skirmishes in the Anglo-Satsuma (1863) and Shimonoseki wars of 1864. This was a contributing factor in the overthrow of the Tokugawa Shogunate and the Meiji Restoration of 1868. (It would be seven decades until their next fight in Dec 1941!) British naval instructors began arriving in 1864; the IJN had many British- built ships; it learnt tactics and strategy from numerous RN officers; British princes serving in ships called on Japanese royalty. If today navies exchange communication equipment (sometimes called fly-away kits) between ships during multi-national exercises, it is well to remember that in 1902, Admiral Jackie Fisher, as CINC, Mediterranean fleet gave similar equipment to IJN ships at Malta which they used in European waters and later bought. Good wireless radios were instrumental in their victories at Port Arthur and Tsushima. It is also of interest to us in India that, in

1903, the Japanese GHQ appointed an Army attaché in Delhi.[12] This is a small example to show that Tokyo was a serious player alright. The big-ticket item linking Japan to India was the understanding within the Anglo-Japanese alliance that the IJ Army would assist India in case of a war with Russia in the NWFP. [13] This clause was removed only in 1911 when the Treaty was renegotiated. Admiral Jellicoe, the First Sea Lord, on a visit to India in 1919 found the mood in the ruling class decidedly anti-Japanese. (Japan had been suspected, with some reason but more exaggeration, to give support to Indian freedom fighters.) Jellicoe presciently wrote in his report, "Japan as the nation from which trouble might conceivably arrive in the future" and strongly recommended the creation of a Far-East fleet based at Singapore.[14] Curzon, as the Foreign Secretary in 1920 was even more explicit, and insightful:

"A hostile and suspicious Japan may be a great nuisance–in China, in India, in the Far East generally. As it is, we can keep a watch on her intrigues, mitigate her aggressions and from time to time obtain useful support."[15]

From an American perspective today, would it be a reasonable analogy to substitute China for Japan and vice-versa in Curzon's statement?

Time prevents us from going deeper into Indo-Pacific connections during WW I. Not only the war, but its aftermath continued to knit together strategic concerns of many powers; of growing ambitions; of growing trade; of greater thirst for resources; of domestic political turmoil; of freedom struggles; and, as always, there were the considerations of Fear, Honour and Interests.

Time also prevents us from going into details of the Washington Conference of Nov 1921 where two global powers, Britain and the US

---

12 Phillips O'Brien,ed. *The Anglo- Japanese Alliance 1902-1922.* Routledge Curzon (London) 2004, p 71. This book has very useful chapters that cover all aspects of this alliance from the Japanese, British, Australian, Indian and US perspectives. It neither over interprets nor over simplifies the alliance

13 Ibid, p 71.

14 Ibid, p 244. The chapter, titled " *India, pan-Asianism and the Anglo- Japanese Alliance*" by Anthony Best would be of special interest to Indian policy makers and scholars.

15 Ibid, p 245.

and a new entrant to the high table, Japan met to discuss limitations on naval shipbuilding and, indeed, a ten- year "holiday" in capital ship construction. There were larger groupings in the Four-Power Pact and Nine-Power Treaty. At one level, these could be called successful; at another, almost eyewash. France, fearing Germany, would not agree to inclusion of limitations on Armies and Air Forces. Japan was unhappy at having to agree to respect China's territorial integrity. American officers were unhappy that the cuts gave Japan relative superiority where it mattered most, in the Pacific; and, Britannia was unhappy at its declining ability to rule the waves. Although recent allies, US and Britain continued to see each other in somewhat adversarial terms mainly on the question of who would rule the waves. In later years, the friendship grew but ever so slowly. New regimes in Italy and Germany, a new aggressiveness and ambitions of Japan, and growing fears of the Anglo- Saxon world saw to the demise of any lasting success of such arms limitation treaties.

Soon after the fall of France to Germany, the Japanese foreign minister, Matsuoka Yosuke announced in Aug 1940 the government's policy of forming a "Greater East Asia Co-Prosperity Sphere". In some ways this was an oriental Monroe Doctrine with shades of 'Lebensraum'. By June 1940 Japan had occupied French Indo-China repeating its moves against German colonies in the previous war. By Sep that year, the Tripartite Pact was in place. Japan now began experiencing some constraints of US sanctions. Plans for war with the US and UK, as well as the impact of sanctions both underscored the need for tapping into the vast resources of their envisaged empire. In the 1930's, Japanese technocrats had seen the potential of minerals that they could extract from the sea bed of the Southern seas is, much as is happening today. A Japanese version of the Molotov- Ribbentrop pact increased Tokyo's confidence of attaining its objectives in the war of choice that it wanted to embark upon. George Baer summed the US dilemma well: "The US could not stand by if its declared interests were imperilled, yet—and here was the problem—it was not ready to defend them."[16] This could well be its current dilemma

---

16 George Baer. *One Hundred Years of Sea Power 1890-1990*. Stanford (1993), p. 153. The book has an excellent chapter, *"Are We Ready? 1938-1940"*. US Navy position papers candidly highlighted its un- preparedness as well as the strategies and contradictions of the Atlantic and Pacific theatres.

and the shared fears of its East Asian and Antipodean allies.

We need not dwell much further on the Indo-Pacific dynamics of the Second World War, or the Cold War. The Korean and Vietnamese wars and their consequences could, in the context of this presentation, be summarised as follows:-

(a) To some extent, the unitarian consideration of the Indo-Pacific declined for all players in the 1970s and '80s. The US as well as the Soviet Union made forays into the IO, but their major strategic considerations remained in the Atlantic and Pacific oceans.

(b) A worn-out US retreated, but did not let go of a base like Diego Garcia. It fulfils their strategic needs and interests to this day. But, it also built up its old connections with China in the Nixon-Kissinger period against USSR.

(c) With alacrity and strategic foresight, the Chinese moved in quickly into the wakes left by US Navy ships and seized what it could from South Vietnam, in the battle of the Paracel Islands on 19 Jan 1974. Understandably, its ostensible friend, North Vietnam, was not amused! Its future honour and interests as a united Vietnam were already dear to them.

(d) The economic significance and clout of the ASEAN, later the APEC, ARF and its variants once again made old players like the US and new majors like China and India look at the broader connections and emerging concerns of the Asia- Pacific. It also brought to the fore the role that the two oceans, and the seas within, play as highways to be accessed and perhaps sometimes contested.

(e) The growth of China, the complex global economic connections and entanglements are also well appreciated. These make the desired outcomes from the use of force to redeem honour, further interests, or exploit fears hard to predict. The amount of trade or even FDI that some countries have in China could be a dampener of sorts for conflict, but not a guarantee for perennial peace. It remains of interest to us that trade between Germany and Britain in the years preceding WW I was very high; they had military interaction and a small aside, Germany had sent ships to the British naval review in 1911!

(f) The problem in making strategic forecasts often is in inferences being mistaken for conclusions. This is not new. Peace or the un-likelihood of war has been predicted in the past. In response to a question in 1924 on the possibility of war between Japan and England, Churchill famously said, "I do not believe there is the slightest chance of it in our lifetime."[17] Contrast this with what Admirals Jellicoe and his successor, David Beatty had said in the very same times.

(g) Experts sometimes say that today's competition is about economics, not empires, about cooperation not confrontation. The evidence of the past few centuries does suggest that competition has primarily been about creating economic benefit. Specifically in the case of the Asia-Pacific or the Indo-Pacific in the past 250 years, commercial interests, and the desire to do better for one's own people has been a very important driver. Access to markets, with or without territorial conquest, were ever-present factors. If this was to be done at the expense of other peoples, it was taken in stride. One agrees that today it has become a little more difficult to resort to war as an instrument of policy; the risks for favourable strategic outcomes and unintended consequences are higher.

(h) Nonetheless, strategic assessments of complex and competing factors of fear, honour and interests can be made and will be made. Who is to say that no nation is likely to make a major show of force or use of force to reclaim territory or islands it says are matters of honour?

(j) Could the space created by appeasement be exploited adroitly by an "appease"? It has happened in the past, and who is to say it won't in the future?

(k) Therefore, how different in fundamental nature, even if not in technological character, is the perceived need by so many

---

17 Max Boot. *War made New: Technology Warfare, and the Course of History, 1500 to Today*. Gotham (New York) 2006, p.255.

nations in the Indo- Pacific to equip themselves militarily and/or via alliances or special relationships compared to the decades we have examined? Here, Clausewitz's observation seems particularly astute:-

"The aggressor is always peace-loving (as Bonaparte always claimed to be); he would prefer to take over the country unopposed. To prevent his doing so one must be willing to make war and be prepared for it. In other words it is the weak, those most likely to need defence, who should always be armed in order not to be overwhelmed."[18]

(l) There is enough recent commentary on the so-called Thucydides trap. Thucydides had said, "It was the rise of Athens and the fear that inspired in Sparta, that made war inevitable."[19] As Allison puts it, "The metaphor reminds us of the dangers two parties face when a rising power rivals a ruling power."[20] This writer feels that while such a trap is simply not inevitable, we should never ignore the significance of fear, honour and interest.

(m) Two large powers may become embroiled due to relatively small sparks, whether the specific cause was reason, a ruse, or an excuse. The raising of temperatures between actors in the current maritime disputes in the Far Eastern seas, combined with some economic crisis, cyber-attack, an accident or incident involving military units and personnel, internal domestic turmoil could form combinations that could be difficult to control. It is sobering to remember that a terrorist's bullet in Sarajevo on 28 June 1914, led to the "Guns of August" and "The March of Folly".[21]

In this welter and uncertainty, prudence and pragmatism may give way to the use of force in a manner not seen in the last decade or so. As in periods past, the default risk-mitigation strategy for most

---

18 Clausewitz. *On War.* Howard and Paret, p. 370.

19 Robert Zoellick, "US China and Thucydides", The National Interest, Jul- Aug 2013.

20 Graham Allison, "Thucydides' Trap has been Sprung in the Pacific", Financial Times, 21 Aug 2012.

21 Both are titles of famous books by celebrated historian, Barbara Tuchman.

players might be to continue enhancing their war-fighting capabilities and using other politico-diplomatic means so that these capabilities might not need to be put to test.

Retrospect may help us with prospect, even if the past is rarely a mirror to the future. Hindsight from succeeding generations may well prove that Thucydides was wrong; foresight in our own generation would do well to assume that he could continue to be right and that competing fears, honour and interests would need to be watched rather carefully.

Will the many ships-of-state manoeuvreing in the Indo-Pacific occasionally glance astern into their wakes while closely watching what their bow waves might uncover or bows encounter? Colin Gray's advice, "surprises happen" may be a good warning to hang on the bridge![22]

---

22 Colin Gray. *How has War Changed Since the End of the Cold War?* Parameters, US Army War College, Spring 2005, p. 17

Session - II

Discussion

Issue Raised

How do you see India's role in the Indo Pacific region?

Response

Close cooperation between India-Japan-US and expansion of this partnership in the maritime domain will be a good idea. We need the US nuclear umbrella in the South China Sea. India can also have its nuclear umbrella there to ensure freedom of navigation and ensure peace in the South China Sea.

Issue Raised

What is the potential for India-Japan-US partnership in the IPR?

Response

India, Japan and the US have a large potential market and if we can keep peace in that entire area, it will be good for the entire world economy including the Chinese who we welcome to be a member of that economic partnership. If we do too much or if we are too strong maritime powers, I think there is no danger in that. But if we do too little, we can tempt somebody to interrupt in the region. I hope these are not unrealistic ideas about what Indo-Japan-US partnership should be.

Session - II

Chairman's Concluding Remarks

Vice Admiral Arun Kumar Singh, PVSM, AVSM, NM (Retd)

I have heard of battle fatigue but did not know there is seminar fatigue. There were only two questions. Everyone seems so crystal clear about the papers presented. We now come to the end of the session and I thank the panel for presenting their views.

SESSION - III

EVOLVING POLITICO-SECURITY, ECONOMIC AND MARITIME CHALLENGES

Chairman	Rear Admiral K Raja Menon (Retd)
Co- Chairman	Dr Tzong-Ho Bau
First Paper	Colonel (Dr) Thomas X Hammes (Retd)
Second Paper	Professor Cai Penghong
Third Paper	Shri Mohan Guruswamy
Fourth Paper	Mr U Kyee Myint
Fifth Paper	Lt Col Nguyen The Hong
Discussion	
Concluding Remarks	Rear Admiral K Raja Menon (Retd) and Dr Tzong-Ho Bau

Session - III

Chairman's Opening Remarks

Rear Admiral K Raja Menon (Retd)

It is a pleasure to co-chair this session with Dr Tzong-Ho Bau. I will chair a couple of speakers and Dr Bau would chair the others. As the speaker just announced, the theme of this session is 'Evolving Politico-Security, Economic and Maritime Challenges'. This requires certain amount of looking into the future and also how things have evolved. I think the stage was set in this area by the government in Beijing which as early as in 1980s commissioned studies on Comprehensive National Power (CNP). Chinese were the first to undertake studies on CNP. Two studies were done; one was under Chinese Academy of Social Sciences and the other one by Chinese Academy of Military Sciences. They listed nations of the world on the basis of their CNP, and also, projected power, twenty years down the line. Both institutions put economic strength of a country as the basis of CNP. That is understandable as you cannot have expensive Navies without economic strength. We have had other studies since then on Comprehensive National Power, one notably by the United States. It did not list the positions of countries as such. It was a unique study in the sense that the US was not interested in the order in which nations would appear. It was a study of post-industrial society and concluded that the US would remain at the top of the list as long as technical innovation comes out of the United States. That was a fairly reasonable assumption.

This morning we have five speakers and I am told that the bio-data of all the speakers has been distributed to you. It is over to our first speaker, Dr Hammes from the United States.

Session - III

First Paper

Colonel (Dr) Thomas X Hammes

"Great Power Rivalry – Inevitable or a Choice?"

The subject of this panel, Evolving Politico-Security, Economic and Maritime Challenges, gives the panelists a very broad canvas, and I intend to take advantage of it. There are a lot of immediate issues that could be discussed, from territorial disputes to evolving economic structures to establishing normative rules for interaction between naval vessels. However, I am going to discuss what I think is the most important, long-term issue that spans this spectrum of challenges, what actions can the United States and its friends take to encourage the economic rise of China while preventing conflict.

Obviously, I am not one of the first to address this subject. As early as 2000, "China's most senior leaders put aside the routine of governing 1.3 billion people to spend a couple of afternoons studying the rise of great powers."[1] In studying the subject, the Chinese leadership noted that increased economic strength consistently led to increased international power, and this often led to conflict. China Central Television went on to develop a series based on these discussions.

Over a two-week period in 2006, China Central Television screened a twelve-part documentary entitled "The Rise of the Great Powers" during prime time. Scholars from abroad such as Yale historian Paul Kennedy appeared in the series, which examined the history of nine great powers—Portugal, Spain, the Netherlands, Great Britain, France, Germany, Japan, Russia, and the United States. The documentary gave particular attention to Japan, the first modern

---

1 "The dangers of a rising China," *The Economist,* 02 Dec 2010, www.economist.com/node/17629709, accessed 04 Oct 2013.

Asian power, and the lessons of its rise. The television series raised the question of whether war and destruction, which had hitherto been the result of the rise of a new power, would be the future for China. Past experience seemed to confirm such pessimism.[2]

It took a number of years but western leaders and think tanks began to address the same question. In a large part, western interest has been driven by China's apparent abandonment of its "charm offensive" post-2007 and the use of its new power to intimidate other nations. As with other complex power relationships, the opinions on how the relationship between China and the United States will evolve span a wide spectrum.

Pessimists point to major conflicts that have occurred when rising powers clashed with the dominant power. In particular, such scholars emphasize the clashes between Britain and Germany that resulted in WWI (and arguably round two in WWII) and the War in the Pacific between Japan and the United States. In the book, 'Asia Responds to Rising Powers', the highly regarded National Bureau of Asian Research notes that:

While liberalism suggests that interdependence, international institutions, nuclear weapons, and new forms of security threats will impel nations to cooperate, realism holds that the new distribution of power will create the kind of tensions that have been historically resolved through war. Asia's first modern power, early twentieth-century Japan, provides an example of the failure to manage a new rising power. This and other precedents suggest that Europe's history of interstate conflict could be Asia's future.[3]

Reinforcing this pessimistic theme, some scholars point to the millennia old pattern of conflict between empires. They point to the Greeks and Persians, the Warring States period in China, the Romans and Carthaginians, and the British and French empires to illustrate

---

2 Kenneth B. Pyle, International Order and the Rise of Asia: History and Theory, Edited by Ashley J. Tellis, Travis Tanner, and Jessica Keough, *Asia Responds to its Rising Powers: China and India,* The National Bureau of Asian Research, 2011, p. 37, http://www.nbr. org/publications/strategic_asia/pdf/SA11_03_Overview.pdf, accessed 05 Oct 2013.

3 Edited by Ashley J. Tellis, Travis Tanner, and Jessica Keough, *Asia Responds to its Rising Powers: China and India,* The National Bureau of Asian Research, 2011, p. 2, http://www.nbr.org/publications/strategic_asia /pdf/ SA11_03_Overview.pdf, accessed 05 Oct 2013.

that powerful empires cannot coexist peaceful. The historical record clearly shows that great powers sharing boundaries often went to war. The probability of warfare was even higher if the ruling concepts of the empires were distinctly different.

Other analysts are more optimistic. These writers suggest that the integrated nature of the global economy reduces the probability of conflict. In particular, the extensive integration of the US and Chinese economies means that any major conflict between these states will result in a severe economic contraction. No matter the outcome, conflict will be enormously expensive for both parties. Given that the definition of a depression is two quarters with a 10 percent reduction in GDP,[4] it seems certain that a major conflict between China and the United States would result in a global depression. The sudden interruption of Asian trade will certainly cut GDP in the region by at least 10 percent.

They also note that the tensions between China and the United States are further reduced because China no longer tries to export communism. It no longer pushes the idea that capitalism must be destroyed; China has embraced its own form of capitalism. They also note that the United States and the Soviet Union faced each other across the extremely heavily armed inter-German border for over 40 years and never fought a major war. They contend that the analysts who point to the historical pattern of conflict between empires overlook the dramatic change wrought by nuclear weapons.

That said, today's parallels with the globalization of the early 20th Century are eerie. At that time, many felt that economic integration of Europe made conflict highly unlikely – and that if war did come it would be quickly resolved. Yet, for a variety of reasons the continent went to war. Thus a rational analyst must accept that, while a low probability, a conflict between the United States and China remains a distinct possibility.

Interestingly, while many studies conclude that India is also a rising power, almost none express concern about India's ambitions or about conflict between the United States and India. In Monsoon:

---

4 "Diagnosing depression," *The Economist,* Dec 30, 2008, http://www.economist.com/node/12852043, accessed 05 Oct 2013.

The Indian Ocean and the Future of American Power, Robert Kaplan stated that the Indian Ocean "is once again at the heart of the world..."[5] He noted the growing power of India's naval and air power. He believes India will continue to grow economically and that growth will translate into greater military power. Yet, he never expressed concern about a conflict between the United States and India. In contrast with this western view, India's dominant position astride the trade routes between Asia and Europe has clearly aroused concern within China. Despite China's concerns, Kaplan, like most authors, sees India's growing power focused on managing it relationships with the largely dysfunctional surrounding countries and not on confronting other nations. The fact remains that India's geographic position and growing strength will make it a major player in security issues in the Indo-Pacific Region. As a result, in recent years there has been an increasing discussion of discussion the potential for a naval conflict between India and China.

Preventing the Unlikely

This author believes a major conflict between a rising China and the United States, Japan, or India is highly unlikely. Yet the First World War painfully demonstrates that it is important that the United States and its friends in Asia work hard to ensure it does not happen. While no set of actions can guarantee continued peace between China and the United States, carefully considered national and military strategies will reduce the probability of a conflict.

The United States National Strategy makes that an explicit goal. In his Nov 2011 address to the Australian Parliament, President Barack Obama stated:-

> As President, I have, therefore, made a deliberate and strategic decision – as a Pacific nation, the United States will play a larger and long-term role in shaping this region and its future, by upholding core principles and in close partnership with our allies and friends. ... First, we seek security, which is the foundation of peace and prosperity. We stand for an international order in which the rights and responsibilities of all nations and all people

---

5 Robert Kaplan, *Monsoon: The Indian Ocean and the Future of American Power,* New York, 2010, p. 17.

are upheld. Where international law and norms are enforced. Where commerce and freedom of navigation are not impeded. Where emerging powers contribute to regional security, and where disagreements are resolved peacefully. That's the future that we seek. ... Meanwhile, the United States will continue our effort to build a cooperative relationship with China. All of our nations - Australia, the United States - all of our nations have a profound interest in the rise of a peaceful and prosperous China. That's why the United States welcomes it.[6]

This year, Tom Donilon, the National Security Advisor, clarified and reinforced the Administration's determination to continue its rebalance to Asia.

To pursue this vision, the United States is implementing a comprehensive, multidimensional strategy: strengthening alliances; deepening partnerships with emerging powers; building a stable, productive, and constructive relationship with China; empowering regional institutions; and helping to build a regional economic architecture that can sustain shared prosperity.[7]

This effort will encourage China's further economic integration with the global economy. Thus, the United States has clearly articulated the carrots it will use to encourage peaceful growth in the region.

Unfortunately, the United States has been much less forthcoming in describing how its military forces will contribute to continued security. In essence what does it use as a stick to deter China from using force to intimidate its neighbours. Bluntly, the United States has failed to express a coherent military strategy that will deter China and reassure US allies and friends in the region.

Deepening the confusion concerning US military strategy is the tendency of many observers to assume that Air Sea Battle (ASB): A

---

6 "Remarks by President Obama to the Australian Parliament," 17 Nov 2011, http://www.whitehouse.gov/the-press-office/2011/11/17/remarks-president-obama-australian-parliament, accessed 09 Oct 2013.

7 "Remarks by Tom Donilon, National Security Advisor to the President: 'The United States and the Asia-Pacific in 2013.'" March 2012, http://www.whitehouse.gov/the-press-office/2013/03/11/remarks-tom-donilon-national-security-advisory-president-united-states-a, accessed 09 Oct 2013.

Point-of-Departure Operational Concept expressed the US military strategy for a conflict with China. The initial paper postulated that in the "unthinkable" case of a war with China, US efforts ASB would include "executing a blinding campaign against PLA battle networks, executing a suppression campaign against PLA long-range, principally strike systems, seizing and sustaining the initiative in air, sea, space and cyber domains."[8] This paper stated it was not proposing a strategy but only a concept for overcoming China's area denial/anti-access capabilities. Published in 2012 by the Center for Strategic and Budgetary Assessment, it was enthusiastically endorsed by the Defence industry, the US Navy, and the US Air Force. It provided both a blueprint for and justification of the development of a new generation of naval and air weapons systems.

Despite the fact it was not an official document, Air Sea Battle created a great deal of controversy. Critics fell into two major categories - those who believed it was too aggressive towards China and those who believed it was simply a justification for the Navy and Air Force to gain a greater portion of the Defence budget. As the controversy about Air Sea Battle increased, the Chief of Naval Operations Admiral Jonathan Greenert and the Chief of Staff of the Air Force Norton Schwartz attempted to clear up the confusion. At the Brookings Institute in 2012, they assured listeners that ASB was not a strategy but was about inter-service interoperability; avoiding duplicative programs; and exploring new ways to achieve old effects. In practical terms, that means the Navy and Air Force need new, common data links; it means they shouldn't pursue similar weapons or platforms and should actively collaborate on the ones they do acquire; and it means they need to start fresh in the way they think about battlefield problems.[9]

On 16 May 2013, the new CSAF General Mark Walsh and

---

8 Jan van Tol, *Air Sea Battle: A Point-of-Departure Operational Concept,* 2010, Center for Strategic and Budgetary Assessment, http://www.google.com/url?sa=t&rct=j&q=&e src=s&frm=1&source=web&cd=1&ved=0CC wQFjAA &url =http%3A%2F%2Fwww. csbaonline.org%2Fwp-content%2Fuploads%2F2010%2F05%2F2010.05.18-AirSea-Battle.pdf&ei=9q1VUoboMe3_4AO48YD4CA&usg=AFQjCNHi9KSB UI_eutv0nsgL5mzxMo4sgg&sig2=pJcJaIXDr4VkixVcH57j-g, accessed 09 Oct 2013.

9 Philip Ewing, "CSAF, CNO attempt to demystify Air-Sea Battle," http://www.network54. com/Forum /211833/thread/1337344866/CSAF%2C+CNO+attempt+to+demystify+A ir-Sea+Battle, accessed 09 Oct 2013.

Greenert further clarified that ASB was only one of several operational concepts nested under the Joint Operational Access Concept. It "is designed to assure access, defeat anti-access capabilities, and provide more options to national leaders and military commanders.... Air-Sea Battle is not a military strategy."[10]

While the Pentagon has stated categorically that ASB is not a strategy, CSBA continues to tout the importance of the concept: In fact, Air-Sea Battle officials specifically said sequestration will in no way impede the development or continued importance of the Air-Sea Battle operating concept. However, its place within the new Defence strategy is still being determined.[11]

In fact, what many focus on in Air-Sea Battle is the anti-thesis of strategy. They focus on the tactical employment of weapons systems with no theory of victory or concept linking the Air-Sea approach to favourable conflict resolution. Unfortunately, while the Pentagon has stated that ASB is not its strategy, it has not provided any strategy to replace it. Thus, the author continues to encounter senior officials from Asian nations who believe ASB remains the core of US military strategy and it includes strikes into mainland China. They note that since China's Second Rocket Artillery Corps controls the long-range missiles, it will be targeted. Since Second Rocket Artillery also controls China's land-based nuclear arsenal, this is a matter of serious concern.

Another problem with a strategy based on penetrating Chinese airspace is that it uses the limited number of extremely expensive US assets to attack directly into Chinese strength – air defence. Further, because this operational approach relies heavily on cyber and space capabilities, it creates the unintended consequence of raising the value of a first strike. Thus it is escalatory because, in a crisis, both militaries will know that the one who strikes first will achieve significant tactical and operational advantages. The only way to reduce the perceived value of a first strike is for the United States to create

---

10 Jonathan Greenert and Mark Welsh, "Breaking the Kill Chain," *Foreign Policy,* 15 May 2013, http://www.foreignpolicy.com/articles/2013/05/16/breaking_the_kill_chain_air_sea_battle?page=0,1, accessed 09 Oct 2013.

11 "Air-Sea Battle Endures Amidst Strategic Review," April 5, 2013, http://www.csbaonline.org/2013/04/05/air-sea-battle-endures-amidst-strategic-review, accessed 09 Oct 2013.

redundant systems that can immediately restore lost cyber and space systems. This redundancy is very expensive and, since much of the US command network depends on commercial cyber and space assets, may not even be possible. Finally, it creates an arms race the United States and its allies can ill afford.

To eliminate the confusion and reassure other nations, the United States needs to clearly state its military strategy for a possible conflict with China. Unfortunately, the discussion within the Pentagon for what is an appropriate strategy is ongoing. Thus, the United States does not appear to have a military strategy it can discuss with its allies and friends.

What Should a Military Strategy Do?

Any US military strategy for Asia must achieve five objectives which are as follows:-

(a) Insure access for US forces and allied commercial interests to the global commons.

(b) Assure Asian nations that the United States is both willing to and capable of remaining engaged in Asia.

(c) Deter China from military action to resolve disputes while encouraging its continued economic growth.

(d) Achieve victory with minimal risk of nuclear escalation in the event of conflict.

(e) Be visibly credible today.

A Proposed Military Strategy

I propose a military strategy I am calling Offshore Control: Defence of the First Island Chain. It does not strike into China but takes advantage of geography to block China's exports and thus severely weaken its economy. Offshore Control establishes a set of concentric rings that denies China the use of the sea inside the first island chain, defends the sea and air space of the first island chain, and dominates the air and maritime space outside the island chain. No operations will penetrate Chinese airspace. Prohibiting penetration is intended to reduce the possibility of nuclear escalation and make war termination easier.

Denial as an element of the campaign plays to US strengths by employing primarily attack submarines, mines, and a limited number of air assets inside the first island chain. This area will be declared a maritime exclusion zone with the warning that ships in the zone will be sunk. While the United States cannot stop all sea traffic in this zone, it can prevent the passage of large cargo ships and large tankers.

The defensive component will bring the full range of US assets to defend allied soil and encourage allies to contribute to that defence. It takes advantage of geography to force China to fight at longer ranges while allowing US and allied forces to fight as part of an integrated air-sea defence over their own territories. In short, it will flip the advantages of anti-access/area denial to the United States and its allies. Numerous small islands from Japan to Taiwan and on to Luzon provide dispersed land basing options for air and sea Defence of the apparent gaps in the first island chain. Since Offshore Control will rely heavily on land-based air defence and short-range sea defence to include mine and counter-mine capability, we can encourage potential partners to invest in these capabilities and exercise together regularly in peacetime. In keeping with the concept that the strategy must be feasible in peacetime, the United States will not request any nation to allow the use of their bases to attack China. The strategy will only ask nations to allow the presence of US defensive systems to defend that nation's air, sea, and land space. The US commitment will include assisting with convoy operations to maintain the flow of essential imports and exports in the face of Chinese interdiction attempts. In exercise, the United States could demonstrate all the necessary capabilities to defend allies – and do so in conjunction with the host nation forces.

The dominate phase of the campaign will be fought outside the range of most Chinese assets and will use a combination of air, naval, ground and rented commercial platforms to intercept and divert the super tankers and post-Panamax container ships essential to China's economy.[12] Eighty percent of China's imported oil transits the Straits of Malacca. If Malacca, Lombok, Sunda and the routes north and south of Australia are controlled, these shipments can be cut off. The United

---

12 Post Panamax is the designation for those ships that are too large to transit the Panama Canal before its expansion.

States must recognize, however, that the dramatic reduction in China's trade will significantly reduce its energy demands. Further, China can and has taken steps to reduce the impact of an energy blockade. Thus, energy interdiction is not a winning strategy. Exports are of much greater importance to the Chinese economy. Those exports rely on large container ships for competitive cost advantage. The roughly 1000 ships of this size are the easiest to track and divert. Naturally, China will respond by rerouting, but the only possibilities are the Panama Canal and the Straits of Magellan or, if polar ice melt continues, the northern route. US assets can control all these routes. Alternate overland routes simply cannot move the 9.74 billion tons of goods China exported by sea in 2012.[13] This is the equivalent of roughly 1000 trains per day. While such a concentric blockade campaign will require a layered effort from the straits to China's coast, it will mostly be fought at a great distance from China, effectively out of range of most of China's military power.

Further contributing to Offshore Control's credibility is the fact the United States can execute the campaign with the military forces and equipment is has today. Unlike Air Sea Battle, it does not rely on highly classified, developmental Defence programs for success. Rather, the United States can exercise the necessary capabilities with its allies today.

This brings us to the ends the strategy seeks. Offshore Control is predicated on the idea that the presence of nuclear weapons makes seeking the collapse of the Chinese Communist Party or its surrender too dangerous to contemplate. The United States does not understand the Communist Party decision process for the employment of nuclear weapons but it does know the Party is adamant it must remain in control of China. Thus, rather than seeking a decisive victory against the Chinese, Offshore Control seeks to use a war of economic attrition to bring about a stalemate and cessation of conflict with a return to a modified version of the status quo.

---

13 "Chinese ports: Throughput up 6.8 percent," *Shipping Herald: The Maritime Portal, 13* Feb 2013, http://www.shippingherald.com/Admin/ArticleDetail/ArticleDetailsPorts/tabid/106/ArticleID/8928/Chinese-ports-Throughput-up-6-8.aspx, accessed 23 Sep 2013.

Conclusion

The most important politico-security issue for the United States, and I think for many of its friends in Asia, is how to encourage China's growth and continuing integration into the world economy while still deterring it from using force to achieve its goals. In short, rather than great power rivalry, we seek to achieve great power co-existence.

President Obama has presented the US national strategy that both sets those goals and sets the diplomatic, economic and political paths necessary to achieve them. However, the United States has failed to articulate a coherent military strategy to support that strategy. It is time to correct that deficiency. Offshore Control: Defence of the First Island Chain is a starting point for a discussion with our allies and friends in the region. It seeks to provide the military component of the US national strategy in Asia. The strategy looks at two major goals in peacetime. First is to encourage China's economic growth via further integration into the global economy. Obviously, China's growth is essential for the growth of the global economy. Thus encouraging it is good for the United States and its allies as well as for showing China we are not trying to isolate them. China's continued integration with the global economy also makes the Offshore Control more effective. The more reliant China is on exports, the more vulnerable it is to blockade.

The second major goal of Offshore Control is to deter China by presenting it with a strategy that cannot be defeated unless China develops a genuine global, sea control navy. This directly addresses one of the most worrying aspects of the current situation in Asia. Like the Germans before World War the Chinese may believe they can win a short war. In particular, they may believe their growing capabilities in space and cyber might neutralize US power in the region. By showing that Offshore Control can be execute with today's force even with dramatically reduced access to space and cyber, the United States and its allies can dispel the notion of a short war. Strengthening this approach is the fact the historical record of the last two centuries shows wars between major powers were long, measured in years not weeks or months. A long duration war means China will have to face the inevitable debilitation of a blockade. The only way China can defeat such a strategy is to invest hundreds of billions of dollars over a decade or more to create a global sea control navy. And even that will not be a guarantee it wins such a conflict.

Adding Offshore Control as the military element of the rebalance to Asia provides a military strategy that supports the policy stated by President Obama. It can reassure our allies that America has the will and the capability to prevail in a military confrontation, deter China by making it clear there will be no easy win in such a confrontation, and finally, it can be openly discussed with allies and exercised in bilateral and multilateral exercises. The goal of the US national strategy is to convince China that great power rivalry is a poor choice. The cost of rivalry is simply too high. In contrast, great power cooperation can bring maximum benefit to China, America, and the rest of the world.

Session-III

Second Paper

Professor Cai Penghong

The Indo-Pacific, Its Geopolitical Implications for China

Introduction

A new term with geopolitical implications, the "Indo-Pacific" has been in recent years attracting the attention of Chinese strategic analysts as well as those outside of China. Australia is the first country officially employing the term in its newly released Defence White Paper 2013, describing the "Indo-Pacific" as a strategic arc "connecting the Indian and Pacific Oceans through Southeast Asia". Geographically, China is not a country of the Indian Ocean but one in the Asia Pacific ie East Asia and West Pacific. The Asia Pacific particularly the West Pacific features China's neighbouring maritime areas. Therefore, China should stress its maritime defence and naval deployment along the Chinese coast as China is in the vicinity of the West Pacific but long coastal lines facing the ocean implies a weak and unsecure potential for its national sovereignty. Meanwhile the Chinese must be pondering over the new phenomenon that the term and concept of the "Indo-Pacific" have been. So much repeated appearances should be of something connecting with China rather than a simple change in a geographical terminology. How does China's diplomatic and maritime strategy give an echo to the new phenomenon with the Indo-Pacific term emerging but Asia omitted in the terminology? Why not Indo-Asia Pacific if you want to create a new term?

The Indo-Pacific Concept Carries a Geopolitical Implication

Like many other countries in Asia Pacific, China has strong historical roots in Asia Pacific and the Indian Ocean Region, but the term "Indo-Pacific" has not been read in China until recent times and China started paying some attention to the Indian Ocean and the newly generated "Indo-Pacific". The term "Indo-Pacific" becomes so new and urgent that even a standard translation into Chinese language has not been generalized in China. Perhaps it is for some geographical reasons. One point is that China is historically a land country in Asia and the term Asia historically and geographical has their landscape to the coast of China but the continental extension to the seascape covers the West Pacific should China have had a maritime view. The other point is that even if China had some capacity and capability to use naval fleets in ancient times passing through thousands of miles of turbulent waters like the Ming Dynasty's Admiral Zhen He, who plied the seas between China and the coast of East Africa through Southeast Asian countries like Indonesia and Malaysia, the Indian Ocean region countries like Sri Lanka and India, the Arabian Sea, and the Horn of Africa. Chinese Emperors in early decades of the fifteenth century did not have a sense of deploying troops to occupy or annex a place at such faraway distance from East Asia coast. The term "Indo-Pacific" must be unfamiliar to China historically and geographically.

So, where is the geographical Indo-Pacific? There are at least three different definitions based on debating views outside of China. One point refers to Southeast Asia-centered waters connecting the Pacific and Indian Oceans. Natalegawa describes it as "an important triangular region spanning two oceans, the Pacific and Indian Oceans, bound by Japan in the North, Australia in the southeast and India in the southwest, notably with Indonesia at its center". An Australian official stand positions this new Indo-Pacific region as an arc linking the Indian and Pacific Oceans through Southeast Asia. Although it does not place Indonesia as a center, Southeast Asia stays at the center. It seems they do not want to include China in a geographical concept of the Indo-Pacific or at least to be an equivocal definition that makes observers confused. The second is that the Indo-Pacific covers a limited maritime space with the partial Indian Ocean and the partial Pacific Oceans. Khurana puts it as the maritime space stretching from the littorals of East Africa and West Asia, across the Indian Ocean and western Pacific Ocean to the littorals of East Asia.[1] What is sure

---

1 Khurana, Gurpreet S., (2007) 'Security of Sea Lines: Prospects for India-Japan Cooperation', *Strategic Analysis*, Volume 31, No. 1, p.139 – 153, cited from the Wikipedia, the free encyclopedia available at http://en.wikipedia.org/wiki/Indo-Pacific.

here is that the coast of China belongs to the mentioned littorals of East Asia, that is, China is included in the concept of the Indo-Pacific. The third one seems like a comprehensive one covering Asian land and the Indian and Pacific waters. Auslin refers to it as "the entire continental and maritime region" stretching from the eastern edges of Siberia southward in a vast arc, encompassing Japan, the Korean peninsula, mainland China, mainland and archipelagic Southeast Asia and Oceania and India.[2] Maybe we can have more geographical definitions from academia and government officials but their explanations and concepts at least demonstrate different horizontal seascapes and probably having their appeals and claims for some special interests behind words. The special interests can stir one's motive to reshape a geographical pattern and it is therefore possible for someone to have a subject map, for instance, a bio-geographical map and even different geographical maps to be drawn up. That is why that the term Indo-Pacific could have different patterns of maps but not a generally accepted definition.

A country that anchors in a specific place on earth is hardly reshaped in a geographical map in spite of the fact that geographical analysis can generate and reshape a certain pattern of a geographical region from a school subject or another one. Geopolitics and geopolitical analysis, however, can have some approach to reshape a political map. Traditionally, Asia Pacific mainly refers to East Asia and the West Pacific and the "shorthand for the wider region of the Asia-Pacific area plus South Asia and the Indian Ocean region".[3] Maybe this is what the 2013 Australian Defence White Paper refers to "a logical extension of Asia Pacific" or it is understandably interpreted as a commercial concern for Australia because it sits between the two oceans.

As the Asia Pacific is the shorthand for Asia Pacific Plus, the Indo-Pacific has been very much unfamiliar to the world for several decades but familiar to the "Geopolitik study", particularly those who

2 Auslin, Michael (2010)."Security in The Indo-Pacific Commons: Toward a Regional Strategy", A Report of the American Enterprise Institute, December 2010, P.7 which is available at http://www.aei.org/files/2010/12/15/AuslinReportWedDec152010.pdf.

3 Ferguson, R. James (2000, 2001).The Indo-Pacific Region, INTR13-305 & INTR71/72-305, The Department of International Relations, SHSS, Bond University, Queensland, Australia, available at website http://www.international-relations.com/wbip/WBlec1.htm.

supported the nationalist socialist regime in Germany, among whom was General Karl Haushofer, one of the most influential theorists on the leaders of the Third Reich. After General Haushofer returned from his Far East mission to Germany, he wrote books and articles in his monthly column of "Zeitschrift fur Geopolitik" on the Indo- Pacific region as well as Europe and possibly he was one of those earliest men using the term Indo-Pacific in the sense of Geopolitik. He supported Japanese expansion in the Pacific realm, promoted a Berlin-Rome-Tokyo axis to control strategic points from the Pacific to reach West Africa. In the 1930s, the Geopolitik was regarded as applied political geography to establishing political objectives and pointing out a way by which to reach them. Since the Second World War, the word has been mentioned almost by nobody but few Australians before the 1970s. The question is why the term Indo-Pacific has recently been a hot topic in the security circles of the Asia Pacific region and what signals it sends to China?

The term "Indo-Pacific" spreads out quickly these days for it carries geopolitical implications. Former Secretary of State Hillary Clinton and her remark in 2010 was the first time a top ranking official from the US touched on the term Indo-Pacific. "We have created new parameters for military cooperation with New Zealand and we continue to modernise our Defence ties with Australia to respond to a more complex maritime environment. And we are expanding our work with the Indian Navy in the Pacific, because we understand how important the Indo-Pacific basin is to global trade and commerce."[4]

One year later Secretary Clinton touched on the term again but stressed to enhance the American alliance relations with Australia. She put it this way "We are also expanding our alliance with Australia from a Pacific partnership to an Indo-Pacific one."[5] Australia has regarded the Indo-Pacific as a strategic arc and the geopolitical and geo-security strategy thinking is clear in their 2013 released Defence White Paper.

The geopolitical challenge has been seemingly deducted from

---

4 Hillary Rodham Clinton: America's Engagement in the Asia-Pacific, Honolulu, HI, 28 October 2010. Avaibable at http://www.state.gov/secretary/rm/2010/10/150141.htm.

5 US Secretary of State Hillary Clinton: America's Pacific Century, in Foreign Policy, November 2011.

economic growth. For a long time, particularly since the end of the Cold War, Asia Pacific has been a focus of global economy and a possible centre of global politics and world history. Asia time is emerging on the horizon and Asian people are proud of the new century. Asia is naturally including India but a specious argument is that India and the Indian Ocean Region have been drawing less attention. With that plausible argument, a new term Indo-Pacific emerges but the word "Asia" in between is deliberately trimmed off. Why can this be realised?

One hypothesis seems, is to marginalise China. With Asia Pacific being central and particularly an "Asian century" coming up, China has been a new star in the new century but the established power must have been uncomfortable and some Asia Pacific countries feel nervous. Probably like Mearsheimer argues, the United States as the hegemon of the Western Hemisphere would mobilize any effort it can to prevent the rising power China from becoming the hegemon of the Eastern Hemisphere. Please also remember the fact that the US has always had an intention to put pressure on a second power since World War II. The US made full effort and implemented various schemes to cope with the former Soviet Union and the confrontation ended with the US having won and the Soviets having failed. Approaching the end of the Cold War, Japan was next to the US as an economic giant and some Japanese elite even mustered up their courage to expressing "No" to the US in the 1980s. Japan, however, finally had to face the consequence of its actions and the Japanese had to listen to the Americans without independence. Now in the twenty-first century China, a second economy has been marked as an adversary by the Pentagon. Even if the US cannot accurately predict its decline in the decades ahead, the United States seems for sure, that it is shrinking but still wants to be in the position to lead the world. The US needs to rally its allies and new partners to encircle China but the first step is to marginalise China.

A new term like the Indo-Pacific perhaps might unite some same-value countries to exclude and at least to marginalise an emerging power China, although it is not effective along this geographical belt with diverse ideological thinking and values. Fortunately, India as a major power in Asia and the Indian Ocean does not go and follow the

US-led track, although sometimes it hesitates. The US is still trying to draw India into a trilateral alliance composed of the US, Australia and India as Haggle remarked at Shangri-la Dialogue last June that "the United States is working to build a trilateral cooperation with Japan and India". As a matter of fact, Beijing does not want to challenge India's historical status and its current leading role in the Indian Ocean Region. As Kaplan says marginalizing China and inciting India against China does not serve the interests of India and China but only lets the United States "to serve as a stabilizing power". Actually this is "a divide and conquer strategy" as Kishore Mahbubani referred to.

Geopolitical and Strategic Challenges that China is Facing

Hillary Clinton's observation on the pivot of history to Asia Pacific can be traced back from the Mackinder's argument "The Geographical Pivot of History". It seems that Clinton was worried about whether the American lead role would be sustainable and survive regionally as well as globally, because a global hegemon should not be concerned about its regional lead role but she tried to use a regional approach to solve an issue about the American historic status in the Asia Pacific and made an emphasis on the geographical pivot of the US in the Pacific Region. This is really regretful for the US and its allies because the US should have paid more attention on its global role should the United States had sufficient capability and capacity. The major stimulating factor is that China has been rising on the global scene and standing at the hub of geopolitics at least in the Asia Pacific. Between 1990 and 2010, China's rapid rise with its GDP growth rate of more than ten percent annually has changed its status on the global political stage. The "Chinese dream" has a target in 2049 when the country will be a prosperous, democratic and an advanced country.

To make the dream come true, China needs to work hard as a country and have a stable and peaceful environment including the IOR being strategically stable. The Asian history should belong to Asian countries and we remember Deng Xiaoping's observation that the Asia Pacific Century cannot belong to the region should China and India still be backward states and not developed countries. China's further development heavily depends on secure and stable sea lanes in the Indian Ocean Region to transport oil and raw materials into China and export China's goods to other countries. China now is a second largest oil importer in the world. Since 1993 when China first time became an oil importer, China's oil imports have increased to be at about 5.1 million barrels per day of crude oil record on average in 2011.[6] The volume of imports is almost 20 percent of China's total oil consumption per year but about 40 percent of the imports need to pass through the Strait of Hormuz, along the Indian Ocean. Chinese policy makers understand the consequence of a sudden disruption of the Indian Ocean sea lanes as well as blocking of chokepoints like the Straits of Hormuz and Malacca. The commercial sea lines are vital for China.

China and other countries in the region, however, would meet a challenge to restructure a regional order through the Asia Pacific region to the Indian Ocean region but a new name "Indo-Pacific" emerged. China's future and Chinese dream will be linked to how the architecture should be organized and how China's position can be accepted in the new regional system. The new geopolitical design based on the Indo-Pacific concept alerts China because China is too weak to meet the US-led alliance in the maritime domain. As this new international system would include maritime order, all countries in the region need to face and resolve a trend issue in this newly created Indo-Pacific region to marginalise and militarily encircle China.

What a trend no one can deny is about the increasing stress on the maritime commons through the Pacific to the Indian Ocean that will be harmful to the region. With the population aging and urbanization increasing in the littoral areas, food and natural resources including water being consumed fast, human security has been an increasing issue along the sea belt. These non-traditional security issues should be managed and controlled well; otherwise they could have an adverse impact on the regional countries and the regional order. A new challenge could emerge out of technology development although high-tech products have improved our living standards. Cyber security and safety could have the potential to be highly disruptive to the sea lanes in East Asia waters and also in the Indian Ocean Region. No country can be excluded and any action to encircle any nation in the region will surely affect the regional environment for national security now and in the years ahead.

---

6 See the US Energy Information Administration available at http://www.eia.gov/countries/cab.cfm?fips=CH.

Any argument or policy should have a sense of diverse nature of values and cultures throughout the Asia Pacific and Indian Ocean Region. A simple attention on a value cannot be an aid for problem solving or a result oriented policy making. The US is using its predominant naval power to generate new regimes and this approach cannot be an effective one. It is therefore certain that the future of China and US relations is uncertain. China is surely meeting some internal challenges but when the US tries to put pressure from outside, in particular, using a new term to constrain China to walk only inside the first chain, it will not be successful. Territorial disputes could have regional impact and inter-governmental relations. In East Asia, an unavoidable issue is the territorial disputes in waters including China and Japan, Korea and Japan in East China Sea and China's disputes with individual ASEAN countries like Vietnam, the Philippines, Brunei and Malaysia. These disputes have drawn in outside powers and the Asia Pacific region seems unsettled. What is urgent now is to find a way out to resolve the disputes or regional stability will be ill-influenced.

Aspirations and Ways to Reach Goals

If we leave the sense of geopolitical thinking to target China, changing a term or stressing a geographical term can be accepted. What is unacceptable is that changing a term actually implies a new intention to mobilize India against China, particularly at a time when China and India are both implementing their national development programs for their own aspirations. Indeed, both countries are seeking resources and probably some kind of competition over energy will be stronger but peaceful competition based on rules can resolve conflicts and the Indian Ocean need not be the "centre stage for the challenges of the twenty-first century".

A hypothetical viewpoint, however, is a war between China and US would occur because of power transition should they be unable to find a way for collaboration in the Indian as well as the Pacific Ocean. For a long time the Middle East has been the American strategic focus but now with the American troops withdrawing from Iraq and Afghanistan, the US is pivoting to East Asia. This new but rebalancing strategy has been regarded in China as a new strategy targeting China. It is unnecessary for China and the United States to repeat history of conflict between major powers but the narrative about the "inevitability" of such conflict has become popular, especially among "realists" both inside China and the United States. If the term Indo-Pacific becomes additional fire, China will be a strategic adversary in the sea belt. As a matter of fact, the US has its own geographic circumstances and it is logical for the US to continue to concentrate on the Atlantic and Pacific Oceans. Mentioning "less attention to the Indian Ocean" will have only one consequence that the US should enhance its naval presence and encourage the US to integrate separate commands in the Indian Ocean.

In light of the Chinese new development program to sustain economic growth and double income in seven years and make China a developed country, China's naval force should be parallel in development to be a maritime power. The presenter does not have the capacity to supply a theoretical or a policy guide to the question as to how to correct or improve China's and others' perceptions on the term Indo-Pacific, its concept and the real intention behind the term. The presenter does have a sense that more the emphasis on the term, the more complicated the situation would be and the challenges in the Indo-pacific region's development might be more critical and negative. But the vision may lie in a reversal process that the success of the June 2013 Sunny lands summit between the Chinese and US presidents brought about. The two countries are now working on a new model of major country relations to avoid conflict and a "self-fulfilling prophecy".

The future would not be so smooth only because of one summit. In the waters, China has dangers with the unsettled territorial disputes, aggravated by historical grievances inside and outside China. China and India have not solved their land disputes. We have to admit these disputes directly and indirectly involve the US and its allies and friends. The Consul General of India in Shanghai told me that India would not follow the US and India has an independent policy. This is appreciated. Both India and China have their own aspirations and managing their disputes effectively will not only promote India and Chinese mutual understanding but would deepen mutual cooperation in the Indian Ocean Region.

Session- III

Third Paper

Shri Mohan Guruswamy

Transition Issues as the Fulcrum Shifts

I am going to move off this subject of grand strategy. Strategy to me is very abstract and I prefer to deal with numbers and facts that I can see. The facts on the ground are that the world is in a big flux. Things are changing very rapidly and we do not know how things will shape up. Economies are changing and groupings are changing. In last twenty to twenty five years, there has been tremendous amount of acceleration in this flux.

If you see the world over the last 2000 years, we find that India and China's economies were right at the top in the beginning. They hit the bottom around 1950 and from then, rise of India and China has begun. This rise has accelerated since 1990. And how these countries will do in the long run and how will they deal with each other will further influence this flux.

Beginning in the early 1500s, for more than four centuries now, the West has been ascendant in the world economy. With about 14 percent of the world's population in 1820, Western Europe and four colonial offshoots of Great Britain (Australia, Canada, New Zealand, and the United States) had already achieved around 25 percent of world income. By 1950, after a century and a half of Western industrialization, their income share had soared to 56 percent, while their population share hovered around 17 percent. Asia, with 66 percent of the world's population, had a meager 19 percent of world income, compared with 58 percent in 1820.

In 1950, however, one of the great changes of modern history began, with the rapid growth of many Asian economies. By 1992, fueled by high growth rates, Asia's share of world income had risen to 33 percent. It is now close to 40 percent. This tidal shift is likely to continue, with Asia reemerging by 2025 as the world's centre of economic activity. The fulcrum has shifted from the Atlantic, North America and Europe to Asia.

GDP growth rates are another fulcrum shift. At one time, GDP growth rates of 2 or 2.5 percent were considered good. Today, India is disappointed if we grow at 5 percent. This started around 1980 when US President Nixon delinked Dollar from the gold standard. This meant that you could print as many notes as you wanted and there was no need to have gold to back them. So, there was tremendous increase in money supply and this reflected in increased growth rates. The world as we see it now depends on credit and not on gold.

Growth of the world output depends on East Asia, China, South Asia and India. Exporting shift is also moving towards Asia. Asia exports amount to US$ 5.53 trillion, Europe's exports are worth US$ 6.6 trillion while that of the US are US$ 2.28 trillion. The US is a big consumer because it has a lot of money.

From where is the next US$ 10 trillion growth coming from? Most of it will come from China, US, Russia, Brazil, Japan and India. Europe is not growing at all. It is stagnating and will decline. Most of its population will be ageing by 2050 and the productive force will come down. Russia will lose 40 million people by 2050. Japan and China will also be ageing at that time.

Asia will have 52 percent of world's GDP by 2050. With a per capita GDP of US$ 40,800 (PPP), Asia will have incomes similar to today's Europe. Asia will also have roughly half of the global financial assets. So, it is clear that the fulcrum is shifting towards Asia. China, US, India, Brazil, Mexico and Russia would be the top economies in 2050. This will be the new global order.

China's GDP in 2050 will be 44.4 trillion, EU will be 35.2 trillion, US will be 35.1 trillion, India's will be 27 trillion and Japan will be way behind at 6.6 trillion. China will cross the US in terms of GDP (PPP) by 2022 or 2023. India crossed Japan last year. Another important shift will be that the BRICs countries would be bigger than the G-6 by 2035. Something very important happening in the US is being reflected in its trade shipments. The western ports are beginning to ship more than the eastern ports. The number one port is Los Angeles which has a trade deficit of US$ 170 billion. The economic development of US has moved westwards and that aligns logically to the Asia Pacific or Indo Pacific. So, I think they have to learn to look at the world differently.

Will America be still important after this shift? Of course, it will be most important country in the foreseeable future. I think 2050 is foreseeable. United States is the centre of innovation and consumption. It will be a dominant power irrespective of what China and India acquire. The US will have ability to influence policy both in terms of hard power and soft power. It will have intellectual influence over institutions, academia and research. It is still going to be the primary country, though; economically it could be a smaller country. In the year 2000, US had less than 5 percent of world's population and had 25 percent of world GDP. That is going to change but United States will continue to be important in the future.

Despite the decline, the US imports and exports have been surging. If you take hundred countries, US has trade deficit with 96. The US has trade deficit with its top 15 trading partners – Canada, China, Mexico, Japan, Germany, UK, South Korea, Brazil, Saudi Arabia, France, Taiwan, Netherlands, India, Venezuela and Italy. The cumulative US trade deficit with the world in 2008 was US$ -7,000 billion.

But, dollar dominates the currency composition of foreign reserves. In 2011, 62 percent of world's total foreign currency reserves were in the US Dollar. It was followed by the Euro with 25 percent. So, this is the United States' soft power. Nobody wants to hold Yuan or Yen as a reserve currency. We all love and trust the US Dollar. Looking at the economic shift towards Asia, former US Secretary of State, Hillary Clinton had said:

"This has been our priority since Day One of the Obama Administration, because we know that much of the history of the 21st century will be written in Asia. This region will see the most transformative economic growth on the planet. Most of its cities will become global centers of commerce and culture. And as more people across the region gain access to education and opportunity, we will see the rise of the next generation of regional and global leaders in business and science, technology, politics, and arts." The US is betting on Asia and we all have no choice but to bet on the US.

Today, China is the number one trading partner of Japan, Australia, South Korea, Russia, India and South Africa. It is number two partner of Canada, US, Indonesia, Mexico and Brazil. Its share in world exports was 2 percent in 1990 which rose to 22 percent in 2010. Countries that sell to the growing Chinese market or are locked in supply chains centred on China see the advantages of maintaining a stable exchange rate against the Renminbi. Trade is also propelling the rise of the Renminbi outside East Asia. For example, the currencies of India, Chile, Israel, South Africa and Turkey now follow the Renminbi closely; in some cases, more so than the US Dollar.

China's vulnerability is its dependence on international trade for growth. China depends on the world for its well-being. In the first month of the 2008 financial crisis in the US, China lost 22 million jobs. Had it happened in India, it would have been chaos. So, Chinese belligerence has a limit. If it disturbs the global order, the losses to it will be disproportionate. China had trade surplus with the EU, US, Hong Kong and India. It has trade deficit with ASEAN, Japan, South Korea, Russia and Taiwan. These countries are exporting parts and components to China. China is the aggregator of these components and parts which go as exports to the US and the western world. China is just a pass through and this is China's vulnerability. World's biggest iPhone factory is in the city of Chengdu. It is five kilometers long and has 2,00,000 workers living there. They eat there, they have cinemas, canteens and banks. China is a Communist country in name but it is the perfect country for capitalists to invest because people are treated as factors of production. There is no difference between a person and a machine. If this factory shifts to Indonesia or Vietnam, Chinese are finished. The US has the power to make this shift happen. All it has to do is to say that this toy is toxic. If anybody wants to fix China, you do not need battle groups. Now we come to China's problems.

It is going to get old before it gets rich. At one time, we said if you have capital, you can become rich. Then we thought that if we have capital and people, we can become rich. Now we say that apart from capital and people, we need productivity to become rich.

Life expectancy in China has more than doubled from 35 in 1949 to 75 today, a miraculous achievement. Meanwhile, the fertility rate has plummeted to 1.5 or lower, far below the 2.1 needed to keep a population stable. Cai Fang, a demographer at the Chinese Academy of Social Sciences, says the country will have moved from labour surplus to labour shortage at the fastest pace in history. In 2011, its workforce shrank for the first time, years before anyone had predicted.

Japan reached a similar turning point in about 1990. Ominously for China, that was just before its economy sank into two stagnant decades. By then, its living standards were already at nearly 90 per cent of US levels. In purchasing power parity terms, China's per capita income is still below 20 per cent. "There's now no doubt," says Professor Cai. "China will be old before it is rich."

Will the Chinese equalize with the West in terms of per capita income? Not a chance. And if you are a poor country individually, then you will not have the means and technology to do that. So, China will be old before it gets rich and this is the problem they are grappling with now.

This is India's advantage as our population is growing. Indian population will be 1.5 billion by 2050. Economically it is perfect, but you have to educate people, give them health facilities, better training etc. China has too many old people while India will have too many youngsters. The burgeoning middle class of India will take off from 2020 and will contribute most to the global middle class consumption by 2050. India's recent growth trends have been quite good and it has a good future ahead.

The last part is oil business. Middle East exports most of its oil to Asia. China gets 70 percent of its total oil from the Middle East, India gets 80 percent and Japan gets 85 percent. So, everything goes past us through the sea. Geography has benefited India and everybody goes past us. So, I do not think the Chinese are going to choose conflict because they have too much at stake in the sea.

Why does China need status quo in the global order? Because 50 percent of China's GDP comes from manufacturing. It is the manufacturing hub of the world. So, China wants to continue its SLOCs running for its trade to continue. It cannot afford to disturb its trade channels at all. The US has got measure of China on this; it controls the choke points in the sea. So, this ensures a well behaved China.

Living in China's neighbourhood, we see that its peaceful rise has become little noisy. It is beginning to jump around and an intense nationalist feeling is there in China. The 'peaceful' rise of China has now become noisy. China's emergence as a global manufacturing centre is unbalancing the global financial system. Chinese hostility towards its neighbours and xenophobic tendencies are rising There are tensions in its frontier territories, Tibet and Xinjiang. India-China and Japan-China relations are characterised by mutual dislike and mistrust. Russia-China relations too have under currents of tension. Russian papers say that 8 million Chinese have already migrated to Siberia. Aging China will also slow down and with this the tendency for becoming externally hawkish will increase. Who does it turn upon? In the democratization of multi-lateral institutional leadership, who speaks for Asia? China is not Asia. These are the questions that we all will have to deal with as the world changes in the next 10-15 years.

Session - III

Co-Chairman's Opening Remarks

Dr Tzong-Ho Bau

First of all, I would like to thank the USI for inviting me to this important panel. Our next speaker is Mr U Kyee Myint from Myanmar.

Session-III

Fourth Paper

Mr U Kyee Myint

Perspectives of the Indo-Pacific Region: Aspirations, Challenges and Strategy

According to the Wikipedia definition of Indo-Pacific, the Indo-Pacific is sometimes also known as the Indo-West Pacific. It is a biogeographic region of the earth's seas, comprising the tropical waters of the Indian Ocean, the western and central Pacific Ocean, and the seas connecting the two in the general area of Indonesia. The region has an exceptionally high species richness including 3000 species of fish, compared with around 1200 in the next richest marine region, the Western Atlantic.

The Indo-Pacific is defined as the entire area of the combined Indian and Pacific Oceans and their littoral nation states. The above-mentioned is an attractively simple definition but the combined area of the Oceans is vast. Dr RM Marty Natalegawa, Indonesian Foreign Minister, at the Conference on Indonesia held in Washington in May 2013, talked about "An Indonesian Perspective on the Indo-Pacific":

"The term 'Indo-Pacific' has become increasingly common in the lexicon of geopolitics. In terms of geography, it refers to an important triangular spanning two oceans, the Pacific and Indian Oceans, bounded by Japan in the North, Australia in the south-east, and India in the south-west, notably with Indonesia at its centre. In the political economic domain, it refers to an area encompassing some of the most dynamic economies in the world, with rising roles not only in the evolving global economic architecture, but also in the political arena as well. The Indo-Pacific Region today is an economic power in its own right. The region has an aggregate population of some 300 billion; it is home to the world's largest democracies; and five of its 30 countries are among the 20 largest economies of the world which accounts for about two-thirds of global trade."

Now we will see what the Indian Ocean and the Pacific Ocean are. The Indian Ocean has four of the six major maritime chokepoints and serves as a maritime super highway for in-demand energy resources that drive the world's largest economies. Almost 68 percent of India's, 80 percent of China's, and 25 percent of the US' oil is shipped from the Indian Ocean Region.

The Pacific Ocean has been the maritime power projection domain of the US for much of the last hundred years. Unlike the Indian Ocean, much of the Pacific is relatively free of major destabilizing influences. However, the far Western Pacific has the major strategic friction point of Taiwan and some of the most contested territorial claims in the world.

The combined area of the Western Pacific and the Eastern Indian Ocean, the Indo- Pacific Region, is home to an enormously populous and diverse mix of ethnicities, cultures, political systems, religions and economies. This region is the artery that carries the resources fuelling the growth of China's and India's economies, the two fastest growing economies in the world today, and in which the US has declared a permanent future presence. Since 2011, the term 'Indo-Pacific' is being used increasingly in the global strategic/ geo-political discourse. The term was first mentioned in an article carried in the January 2007 issue of the Strategic Analysis journal (Routledge/ IDSA) titled 'Security of Sea Lines: Prospects for India-Japan Cooperation'. In the article, the term 'Indo-Pacific' refers to the maritime space stretching from the littorals of East Africa and West Asia, across the Indian Ocean and western Pacific Ocean, to the littorals of East Asia. Some recalled that the terminology was coined by the United States as Hillary Clinton first used it in October 2010.

The spirit of the term was picked up by Japan's Prime Minister Shinzo Abe, as reflected in his speech to the Indian Parliament in August 2007 that talked about the "Confluence of the Indian and Pacific Oceans" as "the dynamic coupling as seas of freedom and of prosperity" in the "broader Asia". Canberra's 2013 Defence White

Paper (WP), launched by Prime Minister Julia Gillard in May 2013 says, a new "Indo-Pacific strategic arc" is connecting the Indian and Pacific Oceans through Southeast Asia. This new framework is forged by several factors: notably the massive growth in trade, energy and investment flows between East Asia and the Indian Ocean rim, and the rise of India as an important strategic, economic and diplomatic power beyond South Asia.

Some analysts hold the view that 'major powers such as the United States, China and India may consider the Indo-Pacific Region as a strategic intersection. According to them, the US, China and India have all declared, through strategy, an intent to remain diplomatically, economically and militarily engaged in the region. One analyst observes that the extent to which they are in coalition, co-existence or they clash in the region could set the agenda for global security in what many nations have dubbed the 'Asian Century'. It may be that 'there are points of national strategic intersection between the three nations (US, China and India) in this Indo-Pacific 'strategic triangle'. In my view, Australia, Japan, South Korea, Malaysia, Singapore and Vietnam are, amongst others, also important stakeholders and players in this Indo-Pacific Region.

Being one of the important countries of Indo-Pacific region, Indian analysts are keenly interested in the development of the region. One Indian analyst has observed that "there are three distinct ways of approaching the Indo-Pacific concept". The first accepts the notion of the Indo-Pacific and sees it 'as a way to bring about a change in the direction of Indian foreign policy'. Analysts like Bramha Chellaney want India to abandon its traditional non-aligned stance, or see China as a strategic threat, promote a vision of the Indo-Pacific in which India, together with the democracies of the region, the United States, Australia and Japan, take the lead in shaping the economic and security architecture of the region.

The second approach rejects the Indo-Pacific idea on the basis that it is potentially detrimental to India's foreign policy goals. Commentators like D Gnanagurunathan express scepticism about Indo-Pacific regionalism. They argue that adopting the 'Indo-Pacific' terminology is unnecessary, and could mean that India would be aligned too closely with American interests. In their view, the maintenance of India's autonomy to decide which countries to engage with is integral to its foreign policy interests. They argue: India's strategic objectives are best met through engagement with countries in the region through forums such as the East Asia Summit and ASEAN, rather than new military partnerships.

A third approach seeks to appropriate Indo-Pacific regionalism to further domestic economic imperatives, while upholding existing foreign policy traditions. It is viewed that the Indo-Pacific concept should be employed in such a way that it retains a focus on 'non-alignment', or 'strategic autonomy', and prioritizes the creation of a stable regional environment that will help build key trade and investment linkages for India's domestic economic development.

So far, for India, the question is: whether focus of India should confine to a top-down structure built on multilateral institutions/alliances or bottom-up, issue-driven regional cooperative arrangements, together with a broad collection of 'strategic partnerships' with individual countries? Some analysts prefer the latter approach as they view it as a key to facilitating the growing economic linkages across the Indo-Pacific, and to managing the security challenges from non-traditional sources as they are posing a significant challenge to India's economic development. It is viewed that India's maritime trade in resources across both the Indian and western Pacific Oceans is of great importance, and this has resulted in a focus on securing sea-lanes and maritime governance through regional initiatives such as the Regional Cooperation Agreement on Combating Piracy and Armed Robbery against Ships in Asia.

India is viewed even by some Indian analysts as falling well short of global power status. Given India's policy of peaceful coexistence, preoccupation with internal and border security against its traditional enemies, and a lack of grand strategy, it is unsurprising that 'the development and employment of India's military capability is not aligned with its overall national objectives'.

India has some of the largest individual military services, and the fourth largest overall military, in the world, behind that of both the US and China. An increased regional naval presence will be important if India is to press its regional leadership credentials and military power, particularly given the string of Chinese maritime refueling bases spread across the Indian Ocean littoral region through to Pakistan. India is concerned that this 'String of Pearls', is part of a Chinese containment strategy aimed at nullifying its regional power ambitions, and regard them as one of the most significant threats to its maritime security capability in the region. India remains deeply suspicious of Chinese intentions, particularly in the Indian Ocean, which it regards as its rightful 'sphere of influence'.

India's economy is its key strength and the hinge for its broader aspirations. Indian economic growth has been rapid and remarkable. India began its economic transformation in the early 1990's. From 2000-2010, India's national GDP PPP, and its GDP per capita PPP, grew by 159 percent and 122 percent respectively. Analysts are predicting that by 2050, India's GDP will be approaching or exceeding that of the US. India is currently the 12th largest economy in the world. However, it has the lowest GDP per capita of any country claiming regional or world power status, which limits its ability to develop the surplus necessary to project power.

India and China are prolific bilateral traders. In 1994, India became China's largest South Asian trading partner and in 2003, China became India's largest trading partner in East Asia. Yet, as for many other areas between the two nations, Indian and Chinese economies are competitive rather than complementary. Both seek resources from North Asia, Africa and Australia and both are looking at each other's domestic markets. India has moved from a Cold War relationship with the USSR to establishment as a nuclear power, a burgeoning relationship with the US and a shift in its regional relationships based on a new 'Look East' policy.

Ashok Kapur argues the development of India's nuclear capability in 1998 marked a major shift in Indian diplomatic thinking and behaviour. In his view, it heralded the realization that India would not develop under a utopian world view based on nonalignment, peace, regionalism and internal security at its borders. The development in Indo-US diplomatic relations has been the starkest diplomatic feature of India's rise. The Indo-US relationship has been most militarily visible in the Indo-Pacific Region. The US support has been evident in the accelerated build-up of the Indian blue water naval capability to counter-balance Chinese regional maritime power aspirations.

Mohan Malik contends that the US has 'tilted' toward India in order to balance China's rise and stagnation in Japan in order to create a stable regional balance of power. It is generally observed that India's diplomatic relationship with the US has many agreement points, the key one being management of China's rise.

India has conducted joint exercises with the US near its Chinese border, some in the contested area of Kashmir, and conducted intelligence sharing and naval exercises in the area north of the Malacca Straits. The developing India-US security relationship presents China a major geo-strategic problem in the Indo-Pacific and China is likely to seek to curtail it where it can. All in all, the US' support of India is viewed in order to balance rising China, deepen its network in the region and benefit economically from India's young domestic market.

India's diplomatic relations with China have been characterized by tension over their shared border area. India's Northern border with China remains an area of contention dating back to China's defeat of India in the border war of 1962. In recent years, diplomatic and relationship tensions have centred on the power play between these two rising nations, their competition for resources and regional influence, and Indian concerns at what it fears are Chinese military, economic and diplomatic efforts to contain it.

The Malacca Strait, as a strategic connector between the Indian Ocean and the South China Sea, is an area of Indian primary interest. So it follows that the South China Sea would be an area of Indian operational maritime activity and of strategic interest. The Indo-Pacific region is important to the supply of resources to China. But China also regards it as within its rightful sphere of influence. Much as India has a sense of its pre-eminent position within the Indian Ocean, so too does China within the South China Sea. China understands that continued economic development underpins its domestic stability and its aspirations as a leader in global affairs. China's economic development depends on maritime trade routes, and economic development is vital for its internal stability and global aspirations. It must protect its interests in the South China Sea and SLOC to the Middle East to ensure its continued development. Besides, China does have some clear national 'red lines', which, if stepped over by India or the US, would prompt friction and clash. The potential exists for China to enter a coalition with the US and   India on maritime freedom and SLOCs security from piracy and other non-traditional or non-state threats, such as terrorism.

In 2011, the US President declared a shift of US focus to the Pacific. Since the 'pivot' announcement, the US has increased its military and diplomatic efforts in the Indo-Pacific in order to retain its position as the regional power. It is planning to rebalance its current naval disposition to 60 percent in the Pacific and 40 percent in the Atlantic by 2020. It is also making efforts to reinforce regional alliances and agreements. The most significant shift in US foreign policy in the Indo-Pacific is 'its relationship with India'. The US understands the dynamics of a growing India. However, India is a non-aligned country.

Some analysts assume that India does not intend for its relationship of convenience with the US to extend to an alliance arrangement. India is said to be afraid that it may complicate its other relationships and its aspirations in the regional security order. However, the US and China are aware of each other's specific diplomatic 'red lines', such as over Taiwan and Tibet, and are unlikely to press each other in these areas. The fear of containment is strong. India apprehends containment at the hands of China through its 'String of Pearls' and China at the hands of the US and India through sea control of key chokepoints along the SLOCs and a maritime presence in the First and Second Island Chains.

In an environment where China fears Indian rise and US containment, India fears Chinese containment and the US fears Chinese dominance, there is the potential for many friction areas to develop into potential areas of conflict. The nations of the Indo-Pacific strategic triangle will need to be careful not to stumble into a conflict born of perceptions and misunderstandings. Conflict is not in any nation's interests. However, it will require the US-China-India strategic triangle to commit to transparency, mutual trust and at least co-existence in the increasingly important and increasingly contested Indo-Pacific Region. The three powers who share a desire for SLOC stability to guarantee resource supply could form a maritime coalition to deal with common non-traditional maritime threats. The three nations should establish a regional maritime task force to counter non-traditional threats, such as piracy, proliferation of WMD and terrorism, in the Indo-Pacific.

Indonesian Foreign Minister Dr Natalegawa in his keynote address given at the Conference on Indonesia in Washington in May 2013 also highlighted three challenges facing the Indo-Pacific Region. They are: challenges stemming from "trust-deficit", unresolved territorial claims and managing the impact of change. I assume that, in his view, to establish a "Pacific" Indo-Pacific, or to maintain the peace and stability in the Indo-Pacific, these challenges are to be overcome. For the first challenge, he advised that 'a Pacific Indo-Pacific requires modalities to build mutual trust and confidence'. For the second, he asked 'commitment from parties to a territorial dispute to respect certain code of behaviour or conduct in the affected area to avoid miscalculations or unintended crisis and to commit to peaceful settlement of disputes in accordance with the principles of international law and the Charter of the United Nations'. For the third, he said 'a Pacific Indo-Pacific requires a new paradigm in the region's inter-state relations'. He said he believed that 'a fresh perspective for the Indo-Pacific region entails one, which promotes a "dynamic equilibrium".'

Conclusion

It is predicted that due to its economic strength, military power, and political dynamism, the Indo-Pacific will be the world's most important region in coming decades. However, the Indo-Pacific's unique geography makes the balance of regional security most vulnerable in its "commons": the open seas, air lanes, and cyber networks that link the region together and to the world. The US, China and India are considered to be the preeminent major powers of the Indo-Pacific Region. Some analysts hold the view that the future of the region depends on the relationships of these three countries.

If that is the case, at the present moment, the relationships of these three countries are not in very good shape, if not bad.

China and India have still unresolved territorial disputes, let alone disputes in other countries of the region having with one another. The problems in the South China Sea have made China and the United States at odds. The return of the US to the Asia Pacific and the increasing the strength of its military forces in the region, and the emergence of China as an economic power and its build-up of military power, also make the two countries not on good terms. The prospects are that the relationships could deteriorate at any time due to territorial dispute or due to some kind of misunderstanding. China and India depend on the SLOCs of the Indo-Pacific for the inflow of resources, energy, trade and investment. For China, economic development is vital for the stability of the country. For the US, it is thought that it wants to deter the possible Chinese domination in the region. The question is whether India also has ambition for a regional power to compete with China and to resist possible Chinese dominance.

However, some analysts comment that India at the moment is not yet well equipped or militarily strong enough to be a major power on its own right. However, even if India has not yet reached a major power status at this moment, due to its rapid economic development, India will definitely become a major power sooner or later, most probably sooner, not only economically but also militarily. But to align with the US, India may need a review of its foreign policy. Whether India would do so or not, only time will tell. Whatever the scenarios, the Indo-Pacific Region needs to be a peaceful region because the stakes are high. It is not only for these countries alone but also for other countries as well as 300 billion or so people living in this region.

To be a region of peace and stability, the major countries should work together to establish acceptable norms and principles based on mutual understanding of each other's interests, and a mechanism for cooperation and coordination that would be able to help amicably resolve the present and future bilateral and multilateral issues, including the non-traditional security issues. That norms, principles and mechanism will need to be based on understanding of mutual interests and willingness to accept fair share of the resources and working jointly with a spirit of cooperation in exploiting the resources. The objective is to work towards the continued economic development of all the countries in the region, and consequently, bring peace and stability to the region.

Session-III

Fifth Paper

Lt Col Nguyen The Hong

"Emerging Challenges in Indo-Pacific Region and Vietnam's View on East Vietnam Sea Issues"

The Indo-Pacific region is home to vast population (11 among 13 most populated countries are located in the region, namely China, India, Indonesia, Japan, Pakistan, Bangladesh, Philippines, Russia, Vietnam, US and Mexico). There are many superpowers such as the three largest economies of the world (US, China, and Japan), three among five standing members of the United Nations' Security Council (US, China, and Russia) and eight countries, which have largest armed forces in the world, namely US, China, India, North Korea, Russia, South Korea and Pakistan. The Indo-Pacific's geo-strategic importance has made the region become the centre of the world's development in recent years. The location of main sea lanes, many large economies and developed countries in the region makes it have strong influence on the global trade and economy. Rising economies such as China, India and the ASEAN tend to compete as well as integrate and link with each other. The region does not only have the most dynamic development but also plays an important role in solving international issues. Despite of the main stream of peace, stability and cooperation, there are intertwined challenges in the region, which have strong impact on regional countries' politics, security and relations with each other.

Challenges in the Region

In term of security and politics, there are five emerging challenges to regional countries' security and the region's stability. Firstly, competition between superpowers is a factor, which has a strong effect on security and political issues in the region. Superpowers' strategic shift toward the Asia-Pacific has, on one hand, created a positive impact on the region such as improvement of cooperation and integration, and on the other hand, made the region a potential battlefield for influence competition. The US shifts pivot toward the Asia-Pacific, China rises strongly and widens its development space, India boosts its Look East policy, and Russia widens its cooperation in the Asia-Pacific.

Regional countries attach great importance to development space in the Asia-Pacific's maritime areas, compete with each other to become maritime superpowers and widen their influence towards the ocean. This will cause interest and security friction between them. Secondly, there are territorial disputes and ethnic and religious conflicts in the region. The region has most of the world's territorial disputes, which remain in most sub-regions. Thirdly, arms race is one of the obvious challenges. Existing hot spots, territorial disputes, lack of mutual trust, along with economic development, make regional countries to increase defence expenditure, procure more weapons and equipment, not only defensive but also offensive ones, and carry out strong strategic deployment outwards. Fourthly, there remain hot spots from the Cold War (i.e. North Korean and Taiwan issues). These are still potential causes of increasing tensions in the region. Fifthly, non-traditional security issues are increasingly emerging in new forms and types, which are intertwined and complex and have strong impact on regional security environment, such as piracy, drug smuggling, weapons and human trafficking, natural disasters, infectious epidemics, climate change and food and energy security.

In economic terms, in recent years, the Indo-Pacific has had a mainstream of fast and dynamic development. Some countries have made brilliant achievements. Many powers have interests in this dynamic economy, which attracts attention of most countries in the world. The region accounts for the majority of GDP, total trade volume and FDI of the world. Most of global resources of material and fuel and many of the world's most important global sea lines of communication are located in the region. Despite the impact of the world economic crisis, the region remains the fastest in economic growth globally. There are rapid changes in the regional context, creating both opportunities and challenges for countries in the region.

In addition, there are many economic challenges for countries and the whole region. Firstly, due to increasing economic interdependence between countries, hard competition between major economies in the region and the world economic crisis had a strong impact on the economy of the Indo-Pacific region. Secondly, the level of economic development is different in different parts of the region. Economic gaps between countries are still large. Income inequality tends to increase in each country. This is a challenge to the economic development of each country and also the whole region. Thirdly, the issue of unsustainable development still exists in the region. Despite high growth rate, many regional countries are facing environmental problems, resource depletion, particularly in developing countries. For coastal areas, many countries in the region have determined to direct their development toward the sea. Regional countries are reaching out to the sea to seek and exploit natural resources, ensure critical material shipping routes and widen their strategic space. This is the potential cause of increasing risks of maritime interest collision. The Indo-Pacific region has many major sea lanes, serving as energy supply routes for major economies of the world, causing the region's dependence on Sea Lines of Communication (SLOCs). Maritime shipping routes through islands does not only play an important role in security and economic environment of the region, but also depends on the actions of superpowers basing on SLOCs. Therefore, securing sea lane' security has now become a major challenge for the region.

Besides, there are threats to maritime security and safety, such as piracy, terrorism, drug and weapons trafficking, human trafficking, pollution, illegal fishing, and natural disasters. Piracy still happens in the region. Maritime terrorism is also an emerging challenge, such as the attacks aimed at the USS Cole and the MV Limburg in the Gulf of Aden, Super-ferry 14 attack in the Philippines and the terrorist attack in Mumbai, India in 2008. Natural disasters such as tsunamis, floods, rising sea level occur in many coastal countries (the tsunamis in Phuket, Thailand in 2004, and Japan in 2011).

Maritime disputes are emerging and will continue to be big threats to peace and stability in the region. Currently, regional countries are increasingly carrying out activities to assert their maritime power through both high level statements and field activities. At the same time, increasing nationalism and internal political instability in some countries will make territorial disputes become more complex and more likely to be a cause of tensions. The region has not had a mechanism to resolve maritime disputes efficiently.

The existing sea disputes are mainly concentrated in East Asia. They are the dispute between Russia and Japan over four islets in South Kuril; the dispute between two sides of Taiwan strait; the dispute between Korea and Japan over Dokdo/ Takeshima islands; the dispute among South Korea, Japan, and China over overlapping exclusive economic zones, the dispute between China and Japan over the Diaoyu/ Senkaku Islands and the dispute among "five countries, six sides" in the East Vietnam Sea (South China Sea). This also leads to a security dilemma, arms race and risk of conflict between stakeholders. Maritime security in East Asia is also threatened by non-traditional security challenges such as piracy, smuggling, earthquakes, tsunamis, climate change, etc. The increasing need for marine security has attracted engagement of forces outside the region, which further complicates the security situation in East Asia.

Challenges in the East Vietnam Sea and Vietnam's View

The East Vietnam Sea is a hub of international maritime commercial sea lanes, connecting Northeast Asia countries with Southeast Asia ones, and is the shortest sea route connecting the Pacific to the Indian Ocean. Among the 10 major sea lanes in the world, there are five sea lanes passing through the East Vietnam Sea. More than 90 percent of international trade is transported by sea, of which 45 percent goes through the East Vietnam Sea. In addition, the East Vietnam Sea is very rich in natural resources, particularly oil and gas and sea creatures. The above benefits have direct impact on the interests of many countries, especially countries in the region, which has made the East Vietnam Sea situation more complex in the last decade.

Besides having an important strategic location, the East Vietnam Sea region also faces many challenges. Competition between superpowers, maritime territorial disputes, arms race risk, non-traditional security problems, problems from the Cold War are still major security challenges in this area. In particular, maritime territorial disputes are the biggest challenge in the East Vietnam Sea today. Many countries claim authority over the East Vietnam Sea and deploy armed forces on islets, which are close to each other. Disputes in the East Vietnam Sea cause tensions between involved countries. Recently, involved parties have carried out activities to strengthen their claims. Recent East Vietnam Sea disputes were not only caused by conflicts of interest related to territorial sovereignty, national security, jurisdiction and natural resources exploitation, but also by some superpowers' strategic objectives for geo-political control over the region.

Vietnam is a coastal state, with islands in the East Vietnam Sea, as well as a developing country, an active member of ASEAN, the UN and other regional and international Organisations. Vietnam implements foreign policy of independence, multilateralisation, diversification, positive contributions to peace and stability in the region and in the world. At the same time, Vietnam tries to defend its sovereignty, territorial integrity with its own internal resources, with synergy from national politics, diplomacy, economy and defence strength. United strength of the whole nation is combined with the support of the international community to create "political advantage", which is the premise of victory. Given the complicated situation in the East Vietnam Sea, Vietnam keeps a consistent view of resolving maritime disputes by peaceful means on the basis of respecting and implementing regional and international treaties, including the 1982 UN Convention on the Law of the Sea (UNCLOS), the Declaration on the Conduct of Parties in the South China Sea (DOC) , the 2012 ASEAN's Six-Point Principles on the South China Sea. Vietnam also supports the development of the Code of Conduct in the South China Sea (COC). In addition, Vietnam's Law of Sea was passed by National Assembly on 21 June 2012. This is a legal document to protect maritime sovereignty and improve the efficiency of marine management and ensure security and safety at sea.

In recent years, Vietnam has been focusing on improving national strength, national stability and economic development. Besides, Vietnam has actively improved its relations with regional countries and also participated in multilateral fora to raise voices contributing to sustainable peace in the region. Vietnam's positive and proactive international integration on one hand helps it strengthen economic and social development and stability and on the other hand actively contributes to peacemaking efforts and enhances stability and development in the region and in the world.

Vietnam's steps and efforts to solve the challenges in the region are shown by diplomatic activities of leaders of the Vietnam's Party, State and Ministry of Defence (MoD). In his opening remarks and keynote address at Shangri-la Dialogue on 31 May 2013, Prime Minister Nguyen Tan Dung pointed out that "ASEAN and China have travelled a long way with great difficulty to come to the DOC in the South China Sea adopted during the ASEAN Summit in Phnom Penh in 2002. To commemorate the 10th anniversary of the DOC, the parties have agreed to work towards a COC in the South China Sea. ASEAN and China need to uphold their responsibilities and mutually reinforce strategic trust, first and foremost by strictly implementing the DOC, and then redoubling efforts to formulate a COC that conforms to international law and in particular, the 1982 UNCLOS.

During the recent visit to China by President Truong Tan Sang, Vietnam and China agreed to approve the agreement on "Basic Principles Guiding the Settlement of Sea Issues between the Socialist Republic of Vietnam and the People's Republic of China", which were signed by the General Secretary of the Communist Party of Vietnam Nguyen Phu Trong and General Secretary, President of the People's Republic of China Hu Jintao on 11 October 2011. The signing of the "Action Plan to Implement the Comprehensive Strategic Cooperation Partnerships between Vietnam and China" and many important cooperation documents during the visit between leaders of Vietnam and China, including border cooperation agreement between the two MoDs and an agreement on the establishment of a hotline dealing with unexpectedly arising matters relating to sea fishing, were a new specific development to solve existing problems in the relations between the two countries in the East Vietnam Sea.

At the 7th ADMM, Vietnam Defence Minister Phung Quang Thanh made some suggestions on promoting cooperation and ensuring maritime safety and security, preventing and managing conflict in the East Vietnam Sea such as enhancing naval cooperation in ASEAN, establishing hotlines among regional navies, organizing joint sea patrols and exchanges between regional navies. In particular, Minister Phung Quang Thanh proposed that ASEAN Defence forces should commit to ensure peace and stability in the East Vietnam Sea and ASEAN members, which are parties in territorial deputes in the East Vietnam Sea and should sign an agreement to prevent the use of armed forces in settling disputes on the East Vietnam Sea. With these initiatives, ASEAN members will strengthen dialogues, reduce confrontation and avoid conflict. These are in accordance with interests of regional countries and are specific legal measures to implement commitments, political wills and the result of the 22nd ASEAN Summit to maintain a peaceful and stable environment in the East Vietnam Sea.

At the recent ADSOM+ in Brunei, Vice Minister of Defence of Vietnam said "Vietnam will continue to make maximum efforts to ensure the freedom, safety and security of international shipping on the seas and continental shelf areas managed by Vietnam. Vietnam suggests that all countries do not use force towards fishermen and peaceful workers at sea".

Vietnam's view is that, the East Vietnam Sea in particular, and the Indo-Pacific in general, should be developed peacefully and prosperously. Destabilizing factors, which prevent the socio-economic momentum in the region, can be completely overcome if countries inside and outside the region attach greater importance to confidence building and view exchanges to remove disagreements. Only through dialogues can countries resolve disputes. At the same time, countries should not complicate the situation. Despite many difficulties, Vietnam believes that the trend of peace, stability and development is still the mainstream in the Indo-Pacific.

Session - III

Discussion

Issue Raised

Do you think that a naval blockade will work against China?

Response

No naval blockade is airtight. The objective is to make China's trade unfeasible. Raise China's cost of doing trade with the world and they will feel the heat.

Issue Raised

Why do you think that China will be old before it gets rich?

Response

Youthful and productive population makes an economy grow. China is ageing and that is why it will have less youthful population in future. So, it will get old before it gets rich. You need capital, technology, innovation and productivity apart from people. China lacks innovation and technology relative to global standards.

Issue Raised

The current financial slowdown shows that it is difficult to make a prediction based on linear data. What do you think?

Response

Lot of people predicted the 2008 financial crisis. The current RBI Governor Raghuram Rajan did that. But, nobody bothered about it as people are moved by stock market considerations.

Issue Raised

Is China different from what it was in past? Do you think economic deterrence will work and China will buckle down?

Response

The last unpredictable behaviour by China was in 1969. Their per capita income at that time was US$ 140. You become unpredictable when you do not have anything to lose. If you have something to lose, your behaviour becomes predictable. China has too much to lose today than it had in the past.

Issue Raised

Do you think China will float an alternate reserve currency? Will the dollar still remain dominant?

Response

Who would want to hold on to the Yuan. Yuan will never be an alternate currency. Dollar, as far as I can see, is going to be the currency we all will hang on to.

Issue Raised

There has been a recent change of nomenclature from Aircraft Carrier Battle Group to Aircraft Carrier Strike Group. Does this have any strategic implications? This strike group was not sent to the Taiwan Straits by the US. How does enhanced Chinese Naval capability of the DF 21 missiles impact US?

Responses

  (a) The change of name is an internal issue of the Pentagon.

  (b) The battle group was not sent to keep the situation non escalatory and yet have adequate presence.

  (c) With reference to the DF-21 it is yet to stabilize as a weapon system. It can be manipulated using smoke, jamming or EM interference. It does not complicate the situation.

Issue Raised

By when will the Code of Conduct be in place in the South China Sea?

Response

Declaration on the Conduct of Parties in the South China Sea was signed in 2002. It took ten years to move a step ahead for it to become Code of Conduct. All ASEAN members agree to move forward. One good signal is that China has agreed to talk about ASEAN. There are still differences on how to make the COC acceptable to both China and ASEAN. I hope that with the new leadership in China, there will be some progress on the issue.

Session - III

Chairman's Concluding Remarks

Rear Admiral K Raja Menon (Retd)

Thank you for this opportunity to say a few words. I think we all will agree that we had some frank presentations. That's the way it should be in a military organisation. There is little doubt in concluding that the economic centre of gravity in the world is shifting to the East. Global powers want to conduct their international affairs through peace and prosperity. They do not want to interfere in other parts of the world and send their men to die in other countries. That is the situation as far as the shift to centre of gravity to the East is concerned. The United States has recognized that this shift has occurred. The US speaker has ensured us that their Navy wants to maintain peace and the world order. World order consists of institutions dominated by the US. China has benefited from the world order for being what it is. It is in this world order that the Chinese economic growth has taken off. Without naming anyone, the US says that if you disturb the world order, we are ready to fight. I do not think the fight will happen as the Chinese have benefited following the world order. But what the Chinese speaker did mention is that they suspect the US intentions of two things. One is surrounding China and the other is creating anti-China alliance. We need more information on this because I am not sure which country made this anti-China alliance. As far as surrounding China is concerned, my view is that the age of containment is dead. How do we contain China when it has a burgeoning trade with the US? Chinese students study in American colleges, what type of containment is that?

The worst scenario the world can envisage is hostility between the US and China. They are the engines of growth as far as the world is concerned. United States and China are engaged so closely and I believe they will not break down that easily. At the same time, countries that trade do go to war. I hope that will not happen in this case.

Finally, what is the role of seminars of this kind? I think they reduce wrong perceptions. There are analysts who still are finding out why the First World War happened because there are good reasons why it should not have happened. Clearly, there were perceptions that led countries to war at that time. If analysts from different countries can get together and exchange their perceptions frankly, this will help in building mutual trust. Such conferences help in positive perception building and I congratulate the United Service Institution for that.

SESSION - IV

INDO-PACIFIC REGION: ASPIRATIONS AND CHALLENGES – THE WAY FORWARD

Chairman	Ambassador Leela K Ponappa, IFS (Retd).
First Paper	Ambassador Gleb A Ivashentsov.
Second Paper	Brig Gen (Dr) Chol-Ho Chong.
Third Paper	Vice Admiral Pradeep Kaushiva, UYSM, VSM (Retd).
Fourth Paper	Maj Gen (Dr) Nguyen Hong Quan.
Fifth Paper	Prof (Ms) Ruhanas Harun.
Discussion	
Concluding Remarks	Ambassador Leela K Ponappa, IFS (Retd).

Session - IV

Chairman's Opening Remarks

Ambassador Leela K Ponappa, IFS (Retd)

Thank you very much and kudos to all of you for displaying persistence up to the very last session. It is a challenge to attend the post-lunch session. We will start by hearing from Ambassador Gleb Ivashentsov of Russia. His illustrious bio-data is given in the USI seminar booklet which you all have.

Session - IV

First Paper

Ambassador Gleb A Ivashentsov

Russia's Strategic Aims in the Asia-Pacific Region

Russia is not a newcomer to the Asia-Pacific Region (APR). She used to be, she is and she will stay an integral part of it. That has been predetermined by geography and history. Russians reached the coast of the Pacific more than three and half centuries back. And it is not just by chance that the East most mainland point of Eurasia is named Cape Dezhnev after the Russian Cossack who was the first European to step there and the strait separating Asia from America by the Russian seafarer Vitus Bering who was the first to sail by it. Two thirds of Russia's territory lies in Asia. Russia has the longest Pacific coast-line.

The importance of the Asia-Pacific region has immensely grown today, for the world and for Russia in particular. The ability of the West to dominate world economy and politics continues to diminish. The global power and development potential is now shifting to the East, primarily to the Asia-Pacific region.

It is the region that houses the world's mightiest economies as well as almost half of G-20 members attributing to the most part of world production including the high-tech industries. It is the region where the world's most important test-ground for political modernisation is functioning which represents not just a pure westernisation, but a specific path of development based on synthesis of democratic forms of government and of local political culture.

At the same time it is the region of growing conflict potential. There is tension in the spheres of finance, energy, defence and environment. There are territorial claims. The region can boast of five out of ten most numerous armed forces of the world. Six states own nuclear weapons. Three more states are capable of acquiring them at any moment. The region faces global challenges like proliferation of weapons of mass destruction, international terrorism and trans-border crime, as well as a known set of purely regional potentially conflict situations from nuclear issue of the Korean Peninsula to territorial disputes in the South China Sea. And there is a very serious threat of internal political destabilisation in certain countries of the region.

Asia-Pacific remains a region where a multilateral mechanism to address various issues of common interest and resolve conflict among regional members has never come into being. The security architecture which exists there today was formed in the Cold War time in the format of US-USSR confrontation. It corresponds neither to the present configuration of fields of forces in Asia Pacific, nor to the tasks of fighting current global and regional threats, and therefore needs a radical reconstruction.

The current developments in Asia Pacific are to much extent influenced by relations between US and China. The rising Chinese giant throws a challenge to the US domination which is met with counter-measures from the American side. The US comeback into Asia Pacific is accompanied by stimulation of the system of old military alliances of the Cold War period as well as by intensification of defence interaction with new partners including almost all states of Asia Pacific.

As Russia's interests cannot be fully harmonized neither with the interests of the US nor with those of China, she needs her own specific type of nonalignment policy in the APR which under no circumstances would lead to direct alliance with any of the rivals.

We approach the existing problems with an understanding that we do not have ideological differences with any nation of the region or serious thorny issues in our bilateral relations which could not be settled through a constructive dialogue. As today traditional military and political alliances cannot protect against all the existing transborder challenges and threats, Russia considers it vital to create and promote a partner network of regional associations in the APR.

In this context, special emphasis is placed on enhancing the role in regional and global affairs of the Shanghai Cooperation Organisation whose constructive influence on the situation in the region as a whole has significantly increased. Russia considers that it is important to further develop the mechanism of effective and mutually beneficial cooperation in foreign policy and economy in tripartite format with India and China. Among our strategic partners in the Asia-Pacific region is also Vietnam which is interested in a continued close and multifaceted cooperation with Russia. My country views the East Asia Summits' (EAS) mechanism as the main platform for strategic dialogue between leaders on key APR security and cooperation issues. Efforts in this area will be supported by activities in other formats such as APEC Forum, ASEAN-Russia Dialogue, ASEAN Regional Forum on security, Asia-Europe Forum, Conference on Interaction and Confidence-Building Measures in Asia, ASEAN Defence Ministers' Meeting with dialogue partners, and Asia Cooperation Dialogue forum.

The more than sixty years old confrontation on the Korean peninsula which has been now complicated by the nuclear issue is the main source of war threat in the APR. Russia seeks to maintain friendly and neighbourly relations with the Democratic People's Republic of Korea and the Republic of Korea and to contribute thereby to settlement of the nuclear issue of the Korean peninsula viewing Six-Party talks the prime instrument for that task. The Russian Federation is willing to promote development of good-neighbourly relations with Japan and to continue the dialogue to find a mutually acceptable solution to unsettled issues.

A key factor of international stability is economic interdependence of states. Long-term economic partnership and joint work on big-scale projects serves the best way to lessen tension and promote trust and confidence between states. My country acquired that experience in her relations with West Europe in 1960s and 1970s. Laying of oil and gas pipelines to Western Europe and West European companies' participation in construction of large industrial plants in USSR reduced mutual suspiciousness of the Cold War opening the path to detente in Europe which culminated in 1975 with the All-European Helsinki Conference and formation of the Organisation on Security and Cooperation in Europe. Naturally it is hardly possible to blindly copy the 40-years old European experience in Asia Pacific of today. But something of that experience can surely be used.

The main drive for economic partnership of Russia with APR neighbours is to be provided by the development of the trans-Baikal and Russian Far Eastern territories. They constitute a huge region which is equal in area to Australia covering more than five percent of the global land space. Exploration of its natural resources would bring results comparable to the United States Westward movement in the end of 19th century if not greater than those. In any case it would surely leave its impact on all civilisation processes in Asia-Pacific region and beyond.

Such a work however demands enormous financial means which Russia may not be in a position to invest at present just on her own. That appeals to international cooperation which is to be based on Russian Law on the principle of mutual benefit.

Where does one start from? While political and military interests of different countries may differ, energy security is one that all economies of the region share a common interest in. By 2020 Northeast Asia alone will consume half of the world energy. Energy security in Asia Pacific is a major condition for further economic progress and regional integration as well as for trade and investment liberalisation.

Russia is prepared to actively contribute to settle the common task of ensuring Asia Pacific energy security. Special attention is paid to developing oil and gas exploration in East Siberian and Far Eastern areas. Russia can offer a lot in the sphere of hydro and nuclear energy as well. One could recall that the Soviet Union became a great power not because of massive oil and gas exports. Big-scale industrialization and the high level of education, science and technology were the ground of her might. Soviet hydrocarbon exports grew manifold just in 1970s when the country's economy had already become the world runner-up.

It is in the interests of Russia that the innovatory development of mining, oil, gas and coal industries as well as power production in the trans-Baikal and Far Eastern areas is correlated with the development of machine-building, including aircraft and precise instruments production, ship-building, automobile and electronic industries, with advancement of science, education and services so that the region supplies the internal and foreign markets with produce of high added value.

Russia is prepared to offer access to its transport corridors, which are the shortest route between Asia and Europe. Those include the Trans-Siberian and the Baikal-Amur Railways which must be upgraded, as well as Russia's ports on the Pacific. We could talk also about new sea routes in addition to the traditional ones via Malacca Straight and Suez Canal. In the latter case we mean the use of Northern Sea Route for transit shipping between the ports of East Asia, Pacific Coast of North America and North Europe as well as for shipping hydrocarbons from the gas and oilfields of the Russian Arctic to the buyers in the Asia-Pacific region.

There are also good perspectives for cooperation with the neighbouring countries in space exploration including construction of launching pads and designing space rocket engines that we do with South Korea as well as servicing commercial space launches that we do with Japan, South Korea, India, Malaysia and Indonesia. The Far Eastern Federal University of Vladivostok equipped with the most modern outfits will be a mighty center of scientific and technological cooperation with our Asia Pacific partners.

However different Russia and India may look, they share quite a few identical tasks. Both are democratic states, and their commitment to democracy in internal affairs pre-determines their mutual striving for democratic ways of handling international affairs – building an equitable multi-polar world order and resisting the relapses of bloc politics. Both have multi-million multi-ethnic populations, both had a chance to learn from experience in Kashmir and Chechnya (better and faster than the others) the deadly effects of such ills as terrorism and separatism. Both are multi-religious states. The followers of Islam account for large shares of their populations and their historical ties and proximity to the Islamic world dictate their special roles in handing such issues as Afghan, Iraqi or Middle East settlement.

India pins great hopes on the largely unique contribution of cooperation with Russia into implementing its military-political doctrine. More than half of the military equipment India's armed forces use these days is of Soviet and Russian manufacture. Just as all other spheres of our interaction, Russian-Indian military-technical cooperation has acquired some new traits over the past decade. Russia has gone much farther than just selling weaponry, military technologies and know-how to India. Moscow and Delhi have been increasingly active in the field of joint defence research. The supersonic cruise missile BrahMos (Brahmaputra-Moscow) stands out in that respect. By many parameters it is unparalleled in the world. Joint research is in progress into a fifth generation jet fighter. In arms trade with India Russia is far ahead of its chief competitors – the United States and Israel. India is the sole country that has acquired AWACS plans of joint Russian-Israeli manufacture, and it will be the exclusive foreign recipient of the high precision signal from the Russian global satellite navigation system GLONASS it will be able to use for defence and security purposes.

The upgraded aircraft carrier Vikramaditya (formerly Admiral Gorshkov), when delivered to India under a bilateral contract, will add much strength to the Indian Navy. This will be important not only for ensuring the security of India proper, which has an exclusive economic zone of 2.2 million square kilometers in the Indian Ocean. Stretching along India's shores are shipping routes from the Persian Gulf to Southeast Asia, China and Japan. The energy security of a vast region of the world and resistance to sea piracy and terrorism are inseparable from the overall national security strategies of the Asian countries and all major powers of the world.

India objectively needs cooperation with Russia in the energy industry, including the tapping of oil and gas fields in Russia and in building nuclear power plants in its own territory. As it puts great emphasis on "naturalizing" foreign ideas and research and development, India has displayed much interest in Russia's achievements in advanced fields of science and engineering and corresponding joint research.

Russia needs sustainable bilateral partnership as much as India. Moscow has never had a conflict of interest with India, in contrast to its relations with the United States, the West European countries and China. Nor is there any risk of such a conflict on the horizon in the foreseeable future. India's greater role in world affairs, globally or in the Middle East, Southwest Asia or the Far East, in view of the country's tangible economic presence in all of these regions and the large Indian community, would objectively ease foreign policy challenges to Russia. Russia-India cooperation on key international issues proceeds in harmony with interaction with the 'troika" of Russia, India and China, and the BRICS quintet, whose members are moving steadily towards the group's gradual transformation into a full-format mechanism of cooperation on key world economic and political issues. Moscow has regularly confirmed its policy for granting India a permanent seat on the UN Security Council and also for backing India's bid for full-fledged membership of the Shanghai Cooperation Organisation and the APEC forum.

India retains its importance as a potentially vast market for Russian manufacturers. While bilateral trade remains insignificant, at about $10 bn, cooperation in industries where Russia still has competitive advantages – nuclear power, space exploration, power engineering, aircraft building, creation of weapons of the future, which work as an external driving force for Russia's internal modernisation.

Reopening of the transport arteries linking Russia and India, the first place the "unfreezing" of the North-South international transport corridor might prove a powerful incentive to growing Russian-Indian trading and economic ties. Iran has invariably been an integral part of that corridor, so joint decisions at the highest level in India, Russia and Iran will be crucial to stepping up Russian-Indian foreign economic ties.

Russia has no hidden agendas in the Asia Pacific region. Our state does not aim to forge covert military alliances that would threaten anyone's security. On the contrary, we look forward to intensifying diversified multilateral economic and political cooperation with all the countries that show such a willingness. Cooperation for peace, stability and common prosperity is the key principle that determines the vector of Russia's efforts in the Asia-Pacific dimension.

Session - IV

Second Paper

Brig Gen (Dr) Chol-Ho Chong (Retd)

India-Republic of Korea Security and Peace Cooperation

Introduction: Aspirations & Challenges

This paper will discuss subjects including India-Republic of Korea Relations, the North Korean Nuclear Issue, the South China Sea SLOC and India-Korea Security Cooperation. India and China are already large, transitional economies and have formidable international political influence, if not yet military power. The achievement of the economic development of these two emerging powers significantly impacts global economic governance. These two emerging states' growing relative power has seen them both appear as strategic cooperators and potential strategic competitors. Furthermore, these two powers' increased influence on the international security order shape their global and regional military influence. Some experts on the two emerging powers describe their perspectives concerning the crux of Asia to include India, China and the emerging global order.

Challenges- China's Perspectives

Wang Jisi, Dean of the School of International Studies at Peking University, argues that "the greatest challenges to China's state sovereignty and authority comes from Western powers, particularly from the United States." He emphasises, "China has dreamed for decades about a trend of multi-polarisation in global politics and economics and that is becoming more of a reality." About the relations of China, India, and United States, he asserts that, "China still sees its national interests hampered by the present system, most certainly because of Western dominance and the gradual erosion of developing countries' sovereignty." He also insists that "China is sensitive to

US-India encirclement, of China in the Asia-Pacific region and China aspires to defy US-led Western primacy" while on the other "Chinese 'Grand Strategy' is not yet in sight."[1] Wang Jisi strongly supports China's 'Rise of the Great State' policy and indicates a provocative trend against the United States, which would bring confrontation between two 'Great States' and change the international order in Asia. This means that there is a possibility that China would bring about an unstable security situation against neighbouring countries in Asia.

Challenges- India's Perspectives

Prof C Raja Mohan, a Distinguished Fellow at the Observer Research Foundation, New Delhi, asserts that "India now sees itself as a 'responsible' nuclear-weapon state." He argues that "although India has traditionally played a prominent role in multilateral organisations, Delhi's participation in a variety of those bodies has not been able to keep pace with its own growing international weight," and also emphasises that "India's positions on various multilateral issues converge and diverge with those of the United States and China." He insists that "India seeks to preserve its freedom of action by sustaining its traditional political equities in the developing world and building smaller groupings with other middle powers as part of an attempt to strengthen its own influence through multilateral organisations." Finally, he indicates India's ambition that "India is eager to use regional institutions to consolidate its primacy on the subcontinent, raise its profile in the Indian Ocean, contribute to the balance of power in the Asia-Pacific through more active participation in East Asian regionalism, and improves its bargaining power in matters of global governance."[2] Raja Mohan explains India's emerging position in the international order and its extended functions as bridging major powers and developing countries. It is expected that India will contribute to the establishment of multilateral peace regimes and platforms through cooperation in economic and international relations in the Asia-Pacific region.

---

1 Wang Jisi, Changing Global Order: China's Perspective, Ashley J. Tellis and Sean Mirski, eds., *Crux of Asia: China, India, and the Emerging Global Order,* Carnegie Endowment for International Peace, 2013. pp. 45-52.

2 C. Raja Mohan, Changing Global Order: India's Perspective, Ashley J. Tellis and Sean Mirski, eds., *Crux of Asia: China, India, and the Emerging Global Order,* Carnegie Endowment for International Peace, 2013. pp. 53-62.

Challenges to Republic of Korea

Besides the emerging powers of India and China, Republic of Korea (RoK) is facing security challenges in the region, which include Regional Security Stability, North Korea Nuclear Threats, International Regimes relevant to Maritime Affairs, and Defence Cooperation. The RoK government has a heavy burden of responsibility to establish strategic cooperation with two emerging powers while securing the RoK-US alliance through security dilemma. Cooperation with the international community to resolve North Korea's denuclearisation is the first and vital challenge to the RoK government to use its utmost efforts for stability of Northeast Asia. The RoK government is also under heavy pressure to develop policies to stabilise the international Sea Lines of Communication (SLOC) activities and increase the defence industry and technology development cooperation.

India-Republic of Korea Relations and Geo-Political Position

India and the Republic of Korea established the 40th anniversary of diplomatic relations in 2013. The two countries have developed their relations more closely from 2000 in cooperation with the 'Comprehensive Economic Partnership Agreement (CEPA)' in 2009 to enlarge their trade scale to 40 billion dollars by 2015. India and Korea established their bilateral ties as 'Strategic Partners' in 2010 and also initiated defence cooperation. Indian National Security Advisor and Special Envoy, Mr Shivshankar Menon called on the RoK President Park Keun-Hye in July 2012 in commemoration of the 40 years of diplomatic relations and he delivered Indian Prime Minister Singh's personal letter inviting her to visit India. It is expected that two countries' strategic relations will further develop through President Park's visit to India.

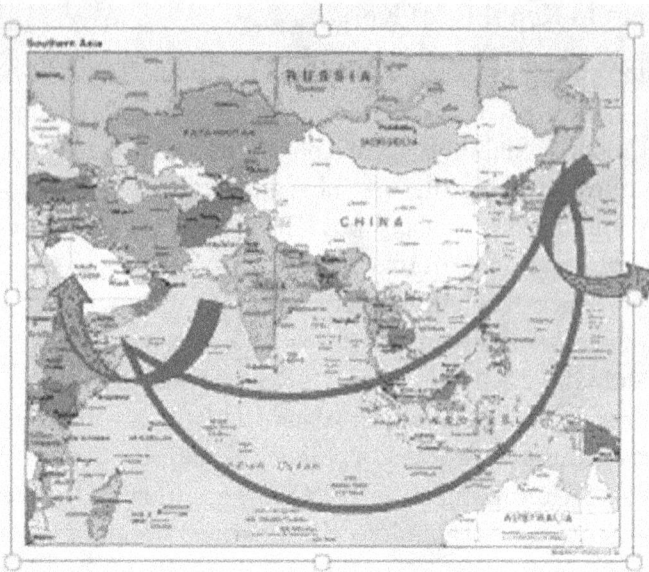

In terms of geo-political relations, the Indian subcontinent, in the middle of Asia and Korea, in the Far East are located at pivotal strategic strong points, which link the Asian Continent through India and the Pacific Ocean. The two countries provide strategic points for transit through the South and East China Sea and access to the Middle East and Africa, and also the Pacific. India and Korea's geo-political relations will provide a vital environment for economic and security cooperation in the region.

Korean Peninsula Security Challenges

The security challenges on the Korean peninsula have been serious due to North Korea's nuclear weapons issue through the last two decades. North Korea's nuclear programme have threatened not only South Korea directly but also major states in the region, which include the US, Japan and even China. A possibility is to anticipate, in which North Korea would attempt a fourth nuclear test in addition to the previous three tests for the purpose of manufacturing a small scale nuclear warhead for ICBM weaponing in spite of international condemnation and sanctions. North Korea has also enhanced its missile capabilities through the launching of 'Enha-2' rockets in

2009 and 2012, and further it is preparing rockets with and extended range of more than 10,000 km that could reach US mainland. This will bring about a serious and critical threat to US security.

North Korea Nuclear Policy

North Korea has declared itself as a 'Nuclear State' in its recently revised constitution, and confirmed in 2012 that it will never give up nuclear weapons. On the contrary, North Korea demands Northeast Asia's denuclearisation to target withdrawal or reduction of US nuclear weapons in Asia. North Korea's nuclear programme has brought serious concerns about nonproliferation to the international community due to North Korea and Pakistan's nuclear and missile connections, and its missile exports to Middle East countries. North Korea claims that it should be recognized as a 'Nuclear State' to follow India's 'Nuclear State' model. North Korea insists that it has nuclear weapons already through a couple of tests in pursuit of negotiations with US for 'Nuclear State' status. Then North Korea may also demand nuclear cooperation in civilian nuclear areas.

However, North Korea has lots of differences compared to India in the perspective of US nuclear policy. India has been a non-NPT state party but cooperative with the IAEA for nonproliferation. However, North Korea joined the NPT and then seceded from the NPT in 1993 to develop nuclear weapons to violate the international nonproliferation regime through rejection of IAEA requirements. While India has developed nuclear weapons for deterrence purposes, North Korea intends to use nuclear weapons for threat and attacking South Korea and US military facilities. It is evaluated that India as a democratic state and a leading state respects the international nonproliferation regime. However, it is not acceptable to recognize North Korea as a 'Nuclear State' as it will attempt to proliferate nuclear weapons as North Korea is a totalitarian state and is under a dictatorship, which has led to become a failed country.

'Six-Party Talks' and Challenges

'Six-Party Talks', a multilateral cooperation device for North Korea denuclearisation, has been operating since 2003 when North Korea withdrew from the NPT officially. However, the 'Six-Party Talks' were discontinued after the sixth round in September 2007 as North Korea launched long-range rockets and executed nuclear tests despite international pressure not to do so. North Korea has changed its attitude in the 'Six-Party Talks' from a defensive to offensive position after its nuclear tests in 2006 and 2009. North Korea demands its 'Nuclear State' position and asked the US to discuss nuclear reduction in the Asian region rather than to discuss North Korea's denuclearization. China has contributed to the 'Six-Party Talks' as the coordinator of the talks, and Chinese President Xi Jinping has emphasized that "China opposes North Korea's possession of nuclear weapons and resolutely opposes additional nuclear tests by North Korea" at a meeting with President Park Geun-hye at the APEC Summit in October 2013. However, China has not achieved certain results to meet the satisfaction of other state parties' purposes for the denuclearisation of North Korea.

On the other hand, the United States has maintained a policy of 'Strategic Patience' against North Korea's nuclear weapon programme, which could be misunderstood that the US would take tacit recognision possibly. Furthermore, it seems like the US will not take any feasibility for military action against North Korea as it has proven its abandonment of military intervention in the Syria conflict due to Russia's objection. All of these factors gives an impression that the 'Six-Party Talks' for North Korea denuclearisation will not be established in the very near future, and North Korea will gain enough time to develop its nuclear weapon programme.

Scenarios for North Korea Nuclear Problems

The above situation brings four scenarios to resolve North Korea's nuclear problems concerning North Korea and United States relations. Two factors are assumed in this scenario; one is the US policy for forcing dismantlement or acceptance of North Korea nuclear weapons; the other is the North Korea policy for increase or dismantlement of its nuclear weapons. The first scenario is the current situation that North Korea increases nuclear weapons continuously while the US forces North Korea to dismantle nuclear weapons. The second scenario is a possible, but not desirable, US option that North Korea increases nuclear weapons continuously and the US inevitably accepts North

Korea's nuclear weapons tacitly or specifically.

The third scenario is the most desirable of the US and Republic of Korea's options: that the US forces North Korean nuclear weapons dismantlement and North Korea takes non-nuclearisation. The fourth scenario seems to assume a strange situation where North Korea takes non-nuclearisation despite US accepting North Korean nuclear weapons.' It might be possible that North Korea would collapse.

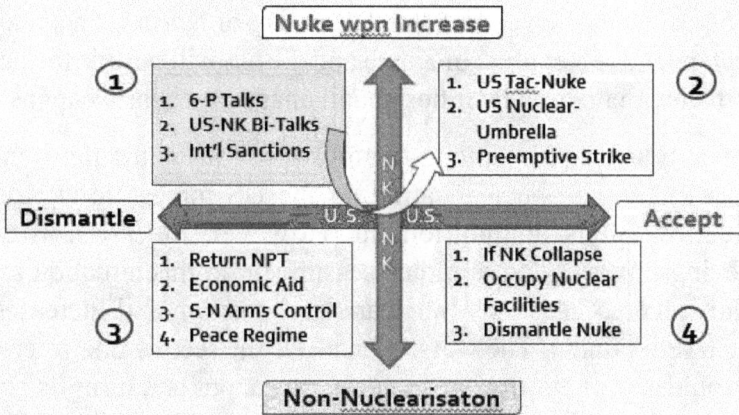

Republic of Korea's Alternatives on US Policy Change

This diagram shows the Republic of Korea's alternatives on US policy change. The left-upper box indicates the first scenario where the US forces North Korean denuclearization while North Korea continues weapons increase. The Republic of Korea cannot help but support the current multilateral cooperation through the 'Six-Party Talks' or US-North Korea bilateral talks and international sanctions against North Korea. The left-lower box shows the third scenario, the most desirable, that US forces North Korean denuclearization and North Korea takes that. The Republic of Korea and the US will encourage North Korea to come back to the NPT and provide economic aid to North Korea. Arms control between South and North Korea and a peace regime establishment on the Korean peninsula could be discussed and then initiated. The right-upper box describes the second scenario that is the worst situation for the Republic of Korea. If the United States accepts North Korea's nuclear weapons and turns its policy from North Korean 'Denuclearisation' to 'Nonproliferation' focused on the Middle East while North Korea increases its nuclear capabilities continuously, it will be a catastrophe for the Republic of Korea's policy against North Korean nuclear weapons. The Republic of Korea and the US should discuss and take particular measures to include redeployment of US tactical nuclear weapons, reinforcement of the US nuclear umbrella, and preparation of preemptive strike if there are any symptoms of North Korea's nuclear use. The right-lower box assumes a North Korea collapse situation. North Korea will be denuclearised despite the US policy of North Korea nuclear acceptance. The Republic of Korea and the US will be able to occupy North Korean nuclear facilities and dismantle nuclear weapons.

The best scenario among the four scenarios is the third one of North Korean non-nuclearisation, as the US forces North Korean nuclear weapons dismantlement. However, the possibility of achieving this scenario is rather pessimistic in this situation as far as North Korea insists its 'nuclear state' position and increases its nuclear programme. The worst scenario is the second one where the US would accept North Korean nuclear weapons and turns its policy from denuclearisation to nonproliferation. The Republic of Korea and other partners are sensitive about the possibility of the US taking this scenario.

The United States has tolerated North Korean nuclear weapons programme with its policy 'Strategic Patience'. Professor Siegfried Hecker, of Stanford University, insists 'Three Nos' about North Korea's nuclear programme. The 'Three Nos' argument means 'No More bombs, No Better bombs, No Export.'[3] Professor Hecker's argument indicates some possibilities of US policy change that would turn 'non-nuclearisation' toward 'non-proliferation.' If the US administration accepts the fact that the US has no capabilities to destroy North Korea's nuclear facilities by any means and wants to concentrate on nonproliferation in the Middle East, there is a possibility that the US would divert its long-standing policy against North Korean nuclear programme. This option will cost us a great

---

3 Siegfried S Hecker, Can North Korea Nuclear Crisis be Resolved?, Center for International Security and Cooperation, Stanford University, 2012. http://cisac.stanford.edu/publications/can_north_korea_nuclear_crisis_be_resolved/

deal of security and economic burden, and also will bring the jeopardy of nuclear proliferation in the region.

India has supported the Republic of Korea's policy on North Korean nuclear weapons dismantlement and also claims North Korea's non-nuclearisation. India's cooperation in the United Nations and international sanctions against North Korea for its denuclearisation is indispensable to support nuclear nonproliferation and peace in the region.

Emerging China & South China Sea SLOCs

China's Emerging Power & Challenges

China, as an emerging power in Asia, expands its influence and military power and also needs to meet growing energy demand and supplies. China has claimed its territory in the South China Sea motivated by Chinese nationalism, and that has brought conflicts with some other neighbouring countries. Recently China has insisted to reform the international order through new international regimes and has demanded 'New Great Power Relations' with the US to create an international security environment favourable to China. Chinese security strategies for governing superiority in Asia and the Pacific are based on the doctrine of 'Win in Local War under Information Warfare.' Chinese territorial security disputes in the China Sea are expanding with the 'Rise of Maritime Power' policy. This has become possible, as China has stabilized its in-land border security through the Shanghai Cooperation Organisation (SCO) systems. China has proclaimed it will extend maritime influence by securing the 'Near Seas' and reaching out to the 'Far Seas.'

China has established the '1st Island Chain' for 'Near Seas' and '2nd Island Chain' for 'Far Seas' maritime security on the basis of 'Anti-Access and Areal Denial,' so called 'A2/AD' strategy for the purpose of territorial defence in further forward sea areas. China has also established a 'String of Pearls' strategy to secure SLOCs for oil and trade dominance in the South China Sea and the Indian Ocean. This 'String of Pearls' extends to the Middle East through Pakistan, which encompasses the Indian Ocean. China has invested a lot of effort to secure China's alliance in this region. However,

Chinese immoderate ambition to control the South China Sea area founded on the 'A2/AD' strategy has brought concerns about other countries' rights of international SLOCs in this area. China's claim for the territorial line in the South China Sea, which has never been accepted by the international community, has also brought another serious conflict in the region. Conflicts of territorial sovereignty and maritime resources competition about the 'Spratly Islands' in the South China Sea among China, Vietnam, Philippines, and Malaysia have occurred with China's excessive forward maritime strategy.

US 'Pivot to Asia' Policy and Rebalance Strategy

The United States has reoriented its foreign and security policy to the 'Pivot to Asia' and entitled that 'Strategic Rebalancing' against China's emerging influence in Asia. It is understood that the main intent is focused on containment and engagement of China through the reinforcement of US alliance countries and partners in Asia. It is presumed that the US has noticed again the importance of Asia in terms of security and economic interests and has perceived the necessity to maintain its supremacy in the region. It is evaluated that such a US policy could be established with the security and stability in Europe and withdrawal from Iraq and Afghanistan war. The United States has developed a military doctrine, 'JOAC: Joint Operational Access Concept' to respond against emerging 'Anti-Access' and 'Area-Denial' security challenges, and US JCS has detailed that with the 'Air-Sea Battle' concept to cover its capabilities to strike by air and sea military assets from far off distance targets.[4] However, the US 'Rebalancing' strategy has brought a situation that has put the US in a dilemma between competition and cooperation with China.

---

4 US Department of Defense, Air-Sea Battle: Service Collaboration to Address Anti-Access & Area Denial Challenges. May 2013. http://www.defense.gov/pubs/ASB-ConceptImplementation-Summary-May-2013.pdf

Scenarios between US and China Relations

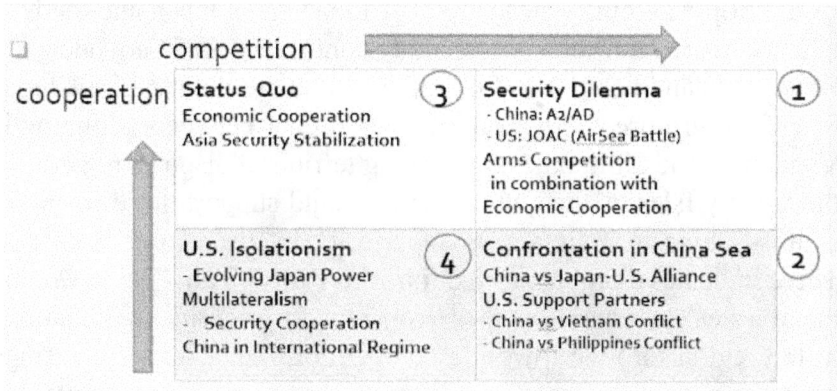

Two factors, Competition and Cooperation between the US and China generate four possible scenarios assuming that the two major powers are interpreting each other as a strategic competitor and cooperator in terms of relative relations. The first scenario is a relation between the two in competitive and cooperative, dual dimensions. This reflects the current complicated situation. The second scenario is a situation where the two powers compete and do not cooperate much while the third scenario is a situation where the two powers cooperate and do not compete much with each other. The fourth scenario assumes that the two powers compete less and also cooperate less, which might be possible if the US would take its 'Off-Shore' strategy in terms of isolationism.

US vs China Relations in Cooperation or Competition

The above diagram shows the interrelation between the US and China in terms of competition and cooperation interactions. The right-upper box, scenario one, illustrates the current situation between two powers where they in a 'Security Dilemma' face each other with China's 'A2/ AD' strategy and the US JOAC. Arms competition in combination with economic cooperation is functioning between the two. It has the possibility of either being developed into 'Confrontation in the China

Sea' or to maintain the 'Status Quo' depending on each state's strategic initiatives. Scenario Two depicts a situation where the two powers will enter the circumstances of 'Confrontation in the China Sea', which would bring a security structure of 'China versus Japan and the US alliance' due to territorial sovereignty concerning the Diaoyudao, or Senkaku Island conflict and initiatives in the South and East China Sea. Furthermore, if there are any conflicts between China and Vietnam or the Philippines concerning territorial disputes regarding the Spratly Islands, the United States would support those partners against China to maintain its superiority in the region. Scenario Three indicates a probable situation where the US and China would make a deal to establish an environment for security stabilization in the region through lowering competition rather than increasing cooperation between the two. This means the two super powers would try to maintain the 'Status Quo' and pursue economic cooperation and security stabilization in the region. However, this seems like an interim process to enable hegemony in the region for a while. Scenario Four doesn't look likely to come in the very near future and assumes a situation that is unusual as the two super powers would not take this option. This situation will come if the US takes an 'Off-Shore Strategy' in terms of isolation. It is feasibly possible that Japan would appear as an evolving power to substitute US power in the region. On the other hand, there would be a possibility of multilateralism in security cooperation to compensate for the vacancy of US power in the region. China will be required to follow international laws and regimes concerning SLOCs and open sea operations.

A desirable scenario between the US and China is 'Scenario 3' which is the 'Cooperative but not Compete Much' option. It depicts a 'Status Quo' between the two and it would contribute to Asian regional security stabilization. However, this scenario does not seem to be possible since China does not want to be perceived as a hegemonic state. An undesirable scenario is number 'Two' that is 'Compete but Not Cooperate Much' to keep tradition. Confrontation of China with the US and Japan will bring a challenge to the region.

China's influence expansion in the South China Sea through reinforcement of PLA Navy military power and conflicts with neighbouring countries Japan, Vietnam, and Philippines will bring security dilemma in the region as US supports those allies and partners resolutely under the 'Rebalance' strategy which intend to deter China's expansion in the West Pacific and South and the East China Seas. Furthermore, if China threatens international SLOC stabilization, it will be a serious challenge against international maritime regime and would provoke resistance from the international community. Japan would be very sensitive about China's activities in the region and will make an entrance as an axis for balancing powers in support of US 'Rebalance' strategy.

The US Asian policy, 'Pivot to Asia' would be in dilemma since US has defence budget problems despite the desire to maintain its influence in the West Pacific and China Sea. This situation calls upon US to rely on its alliances and entrust Japan with the US role in Northeast Asia. US has supported strongly the change of Japan's defence policy into 'Collective Defence' on last October through diplomacy and defence talks between two countries, which would bring Japan's emerging militarization. This change brings some thoughts that Japan would substitute US decreased military power capabilities in Asia and increase confrontation with China's emerging military power. Japan's militarization would extend its influence in the region as much as it has intended through the last three decades. Eventually this change will generate impact on Asian security environment and would possibly pave way for a new international order in Asia.

RoK Security Strategy in the South China Sea

The Republic of Korea has not been involved directly with China and Japan's island disputes in the China Sea in terms of strategic interests. However, the Republic of Korea has secured the RoK-US alliance and has established a security policy to maintain a strategic partnership with partners for security stabilization in the region. The RoK government has also supported international regimes for SLOCs and has developed policies to extend SLOC cooperation with regional states. India's role in regional SLOC stability is very important to protect Korean trade activities in the Indian Ocean and China Sea.

India-RoK Foreign Policy and Security Cooperation

India and the Republic of Korea have developed their relations throughout the last four decades. It is remarkably noticeable that President Lee Myong-Bak paid a landmark visit to India, as the Chief Guest at India's Republic Day celebrations on 26 January 2010, when bilateral ties were raised to the level of Strategic Partnership. His visit preceded an equally successful state visit to the RoK by President Dr APJ Abdul Kalam, in February 2006 that heralded in a new vibrant phase in India-RoK relations. Its interalia led to the launch of a Joint Task Force to conclude the bilateral Comprehensive Economic Partnership Agreement (CEPA), which was signed by the Minister for Commerce and Industry Shri Anand Sharma in Seoul on 07 August 2009. CEPA came into force on 01 January 2010. Rapidly expanding trade and investment flows lie at the core of bilateral cooperation. Bilateral trade in 2011 crossed the $ 20.5 billion registering a 70 percent growth over a two year period. It is expected that the trade scale will reach to 40 billion dollars by 2015.

Furthermore, India and the Republic of Korea have developed foreign and security cooperation through the 'Foreign Policy & Security Dialogue (FPSD)' and the 3rd FPSD held in Seoul on 03 September 2013, which undertook a comprehensive review of bilateral ties in the area of economic collaboration, defence and security cooperation, cultural exchange, and people-to-people contacts. The two countries' relations will be further developed with the forthcoming visit of the Korean president Ms Park Geun-Hye's to India.

Civil Nuclear Power Cooperation

India and the Republic of Korea would enhance the peaceful use of nuclear energy through civil nuclear power cooperation based on 'the India-Republic of Korea Nuclear Cooperation Agreement.' This agreement was signed in 2011 for the purpose of nuclear power plant construction and cooperation which includes nuclear material, equipment and technologies. The Republic of Korea will contribute to Indian civil nuclear energy development through such cooperation, which will demonstrate the peaceful use of nuclear power.

India-RoK Defence Cooperation

A couple of Memorandums of Understanding (MoUs) on Defence Cooperation between India and the Republic of Korea have been established with the initiation of the 'Defence Industry and Military Logistics Cooperation' in 2005 and was followed by the 'Prevention of Piracy and Search and Rescue Cooperation' in 2006. Defence Minister Shri AK Anthony visited Seoul, Korea in September 2010 and established cooperation between the Defence Research and Development Organisation (DRDO) of India and the Defence Acquisition Programme Administration (DAPA) for research and development. A Defence Wing was established at the Embassy of India, in October 2012. The Korean Minister of Defence Mr Kim Kwan-jin visited India from 28 November to 01 December 2012, following the visit of his predecessor Mr Kim Jung-soo in May 2007. The Chairman, Chiefs of Staff Committee (COSC), Air Chief Marshal NAK Browne visited the RoK with a Tri-Service delegation from 08 to 11 July 2013. These high ranking officials' visits indicate mutual defence cooperation between two countries.

Defence industry cooperation is another important area between the Indian and Republic of Korea governments. The RoK government is in cooperation with the Indian government to export eight Naval minesweepers. It is envisioned that the Indian government would consider to hopefully procure Korea's attack aircraft FA-50, artillery pieces and submarines to enhance its military capabilities as areas in defence industry cooperation. The two governments have other areas to further expand their strategic partnership in maritime and space security cooperation, which includes not only SLOC cooperation in the Indian Ocean and China Sea but also missile and satellite development programme. Military exchange programme will enrich the two governments' militaries. For instance, tactical discussions and transport aircraft cross-service programme between the Indian and Republic of Korea Air Force, in addition to cross visits and service activities in the Indian Ocean to prevent piracy off Somalia with mutual military logistic service exchange between the two Navies will contribute to an increase in the security stability of the region and world peace.

Conclusion

In conclusion, the rise of India and China has increased their influence in the international security order and have impacted security challenges in Asia and the Pacific area. The Republic of Korea has been faced with regional security stability, North Korea's nuclear threats, international regimes relevant to maritime affairs, and defence cooperation in security.

North Korea's nuclear weapon threat is the most critical challenge to South Korea and neighbouring countries, and these problems have to be resolved through North Korean denuclearisation. Problems with the 'Six-Party Talks' and US strategic patience policy have been discussed as measures for North Korea's non-nuclearisation. Four scenarios are assumed in the current situation depending on North Korea's nuclear programme and US non-nuclearisation policies. The best scenario is that the US forces North Korea's denuclearisation and North Korea accepts that. The worst scenario is that the US accepts North Korea's nuclear weapons and that North Korea be a 'Nuclear State' in the near future.

The emergence of China's influence and Chinese maritime strategy has caused concerns among neighbouring countries concerning territorial disputes in the South China Sea and the security of SLOCs in China Sea. The current situation indicates confrontation between China's 'Anti-Area/Area Denial' strategy and the US 'Pivot to Asia' with its 'Rebalancing' strategy. Four scenarios are assumed in this situation depending on two factors, competition or cooperation between China and the US strategies. A desirable scenario is that two big powers increase cooperation and decrease competition. On the other hand, an undesirable scenario is the opposite situation where the two powers increase competition and decrease cooperation, which could bring about serious conflicts in the South China Sea and the West Pacific. It is expected that China will respect international maritime regimes through multilateral cooperation for the security stability in the region.

Finally in conclusion, India and the Republic of Korea's security cooperation will contribute to the stability of the Indian Ocean, China Sea and the West Pacific. That cooperation will propel North

Korea's denuclearisation process, stabilize the international maritime order, secure the international order in the Asian region, expand the multilateral diplomatic security regime, and will contribute to the international peace regime.

Session - IV

Third Paper

Vice Admiral Pradeep Kaushiva, UYSM, VSM (Retd)

Indo-Pacific Region: Aspirations and Challenges:
The Way Forward

Introduction

Aspirations of human beings have evolved with time. Today these include education, employment, healthcare, welfare, development, culture, religion, civilisational values et al. Put together, these may be summed up as sheer quality of life. And, friction results when the quality of life or security of one is adversely impacted by another's quest for the same. This truism has also been universal since times immemorial for individuals as well as for societies. It is, therefore, to be expected that a regional level analysis, such as one relating to the Indo Pacific, would present some complex challenges.

The Challenges

Today the Indian Ocean is turbulent on account of three concurrent developments. Firstly US, the principal maritime primate, is in the process of rebalancing itself eastwards. Secondly, the density of China's trade, industrial raw material and energy lines is ever increasing across the Indian Ocean. Thirdly, the littoral states particularly in its east are acquiring capacities to augment their own maritime security but, in the absence of a shared understanding of the maritime domain, such acquisitions have the potential to increase friction.

Particularly in the Indo Pacific region, the littoral states engaged in realising the aspirations of their populace now also need to walk the tight rope between the internal responsibilities of development, self governance, economic upliftment, internal discord, societal inequities, rising expectations, rampant corruption etc and the external challenges of trade imbalances, economic interdependencies, territorial disputes, competition for resources etc. And, all of these are exacerbated by emergence of the non state actors as a persona dramatis.

Uniqueness of the medium itself is the most major challenge. Beyond the established maritime zones, the oceanic space is a part of the global commons. As there are no universally accepted or historically established rules, there is need for the stakeholders to draw up a regional security framework that would ensure smooth, uninterrupted and orderly flow of trade, industrial raw material and energy across the oceanic highways. Stake holders in the maritime domain are not only those who are located there but also those whose vital interests transit the waterways. Therefore, the maritime security architecture for Indo-Pacific needs to provide for participative inclusion of the stake holders in the region.

The Evolving Scenario

It would be recalled that the Indian Ocean Rim Association for Regional Co-operation (IOR-ARC) came into being in 1997 ("To formulate and implement projects for economic co-operation relating to trade facilitation, promotion and liberalization; promotion of foreign investment, scientific and technological exchanges, and tourism, movement of natural persons and service providers on a non-discriminatory basis; and development of infrastructure and human resources, as laid down in the Work Program of the Association"). Meanwhile, the volume of trade among the IOR countries tripled in a decade i.e. from US $ I.1 trillion in 2001 to US $ 3.5 trillion in 2010 and the combined GDP of IOR nations is expected to cross US $ 9 trillion by 2016. So, the IOR-ARC attention was focused upon economic matters in the main. And, "security" was an area conspicuous by its absence from the IOR-ARC constitution. But, at the Council of Ministers' meeting in Nov 2011, IOR-ARC leaders appreciated that security was a critical area that required their attention. And, from its earlier non-existence, "Maritime Safety and Security" pole vaulted to become item number one among the re-prioritised areas of co-operation.

In a sense, it would appear that initially the IOR-ARC evolution followed the rationale and trajectory somewhat similar to that described earlier by ASEAN except that an equivalent of ARF has not yet materialized. It is, therefore, worth tracing that the ASEAN-ARF model sequentially led on to establishment of the ADMM +, East Asia Summit and now the expanded ASEAN Maritime Forum. Put together, these provide South East Asia region the platforms for multiple engagements including a direct Pol Mil connect. Presently, however, the evolving larger scenario in the Indian Ocean Region is somewhat different. The Indian Ocean Region has, in addition to IOR-ARC, two separately taken initiatives of Indian Navy, both of which provide platforms for professional interaction but there are no Pol-Mil connects there. MILAN started in 1995 as a gathering of the Bay of Bengal Rim nations' navies at Port Blair. This biennial interaction has grown since then and last year New Zealand and Mauritius also took part in it. Indian Ocean Naval Symposium (IONS), also initiated by Indian Navy as a conclave of the Naval Chiefs, is a voluntary initiative that seeks to increase maritime co-operation among navies of the Indian Ocean littorals by providing an open and inclusive forum for discussion of regionally relevant maritime issues. In pursuance of the last IONS meeting decisions, in August this year Indian Navy hosted an IONS Operational Seminar at Mumbai in which roles of emerging navies and maritime security forces in collective prosperity in the IOR were discussed. And specifics of anti piracy operations, Humanitarian Assistance & Disaster Relief and Maritime Domain Awareness were taken up in the group's Preparatory Workshop. India also has a number of bilateral engagements with a large number of regional and extra regional navies eg the Malabar series of naval exercises with US Navy, the Indra series with Russian Navy, etc. Admittedly, many of the other navies also participate in bilateral as well as multilateral engagements in the region. But there is no other open and inclusive forum of a scale comparable to the IONS.

The Way Forward

In the absence of any region-wide security architecture, a common regional identity, a history of regional cooperation or any accepted regional leadership frameworks; the way forward needs to be chalked out very carefully.

Where a general correspondence of interests exists, partnerships and cooperative mechanisms are indispensable for safeguarding common prosperity and security interests. These alone would effectively protect and support legitimate activities while countering the threat of current and emerging terrorist as well as hostile, illegal and dangerous acts within the maritime domain. By ensuring freedom of navigation and commerce, these would also promote regional, and contribute to global, economic stability. Accordingly, cooperation and coordination are required on multilateral as well as bilateral bases. A start can be made through developing interoperability in terms of doctrines, procedures, Organisational and logistic systems and operational processes. This would promote enhancement of regional maritime capacities for speedy, responsive and effective HADR throughout the Indian Ocean region. Other benign causes can be progressively added to the list as mutual confidence increases and apprehensions reduce.

IOR-ARC could have been a useful platform to launch this initiative from, particularly since it has a Ministerial oversight. But, at the operational and tactical levels, the task can only be delivered by the professionals. This is entirely doable via the IONS platform that the Naval Chiefs already have. However, presently, the primary focus of the IONS is not regional stability but maritime security. To quote the IONS website "Regional stability would be far too ambitious for such a diverse group of nations linked together in such a loose construct". Unarguably, not much can be done about diversity of the nations. But, the loose construct can certainly be provided a framework that would be acceptable all around. For starters, a handshake protocol between IONS and IOR-ARC would provide a very useful and practical connectivity. And, in due course, nomenclature of IONS can be modified to read "Indian Ocean Security Symposium" for more accurate job description. That would also facilitate configuration of an Indian Ocean equivalent of ADMM+. This is an idea whose time will soon come, if it is not already upon us.

The time is now opportune to rally the IOR-ARC and IONS members towards a regional maritime security construct within the existing framework of the two platforms. Providing a gang plank between them should not be a problem as, just like ASEAN-ARF equation, all members of the IOR-ARC are also members of IONS and the reverse is not true. The only tweaking that would need to be done would be, for IONS to reach out for the pol-mil connect or ministerial oversight and for both platforms to cobble up their rules of business as well as codes of conduct. The former will elevate the stature of IONS. And, the latter is a sine qua non condition because every Organisation needs to have a certain order about itself. This is particularly necessary for open and inclusive Organisations because the new members seeking admittance would need to, first and foremost, register their concurrence to conform to the established rules.

Even as we discuss, design and evolve a security construct at the regional level, smaller groupings and interactions need to be encouraged for two reasons. Firstly, it is always easier for a smaller number of stake holder nations to identify their common maritime security anxieties and agree upon cooperative solutions therefor. And, secondly, a series of sub regional constructs can always be conjoined because many stake holders would be common and a degree of mutual trust and confidence would already obtain.

Conclusion

Baggage of the colonial rule of the last couple of centuries and imperatives of the times ahead, are both facts of life. Therefore, the current task for the stake holder nations is to seriously undertake building up of a maritime security framework, if necessary part by part. There is no template available which can be replicated but there are useful models to learn from. It is perhaps more practical to make a start with the small doables that succeed, than think only big and invest inordinate time and effort in quest of spectacular results which may or may not follow. And, it is important to provide for participation of stake holders who bring to the table not just their needs but also their capabilities and strengths.

Session - IV

Fourth Paper

Maj Gen (Dr) Nguyen Hong Quan

Indo-Pacific Region and ASEAN-India Cooperation

Introduction

The term "Indo-Pacific" was first used in the mid 1970s[1] to refer to a biogeographic region. The term "Indo-Pacific" was thereafter used in 2007 to refer to the maritime space stretching from the littorals of East Africa and West Asia, across the Indian Ocean and western Pacific Ocean, to the littorals of East Asia[2]. In recent years, the term "Indo-Pacific" has been widely used to include geopolitical and global strategy dimensions.

As far as the geopolitical dimension is concerned, the Indo-Pacific region with a population of nearly 4 billion people is considered one of the most dynamic political arenas in the world. It is also home to international Sea Lines of Communication (SLOCs) which is of significant importance in terms of food and energy security for regional countries and beyond[3]. Economically, it includes the majority of the world's most dynamic economies, a combined GDP of nearly $ 20 trillion based on purchasing power parity (PPP), two thirds of global commerce, and three out of four largest economies in the world (China, Japan and India). Many analysts have predicted

---

1 According to the Lowy Institute for International Policy (Australia), the term "Indo-Pacific" used in the 1950s to discuss decolonisation in the 1960s at two seminars held by the Australian Institute of International Affairs and the Australian National University, however, the term was used at the seminars only.

2 The term "Indo-Pacific" was first used in an article titled "Security of Sea Lines: Prospects for India-Japan Cooperation" in Strategic Analysis Journal, Routledge/ IDSA, 2007.

3 Dennis Rumley, Timothy Doyle and Sanjay Chaturvedi, Indo-Pacific as a Strategic Space: Implications of the Australia India Institute-Task Force Report on Indian Ocean Security, Stability and Sustainability in the 21st Century, Indo-Pacific Governance Research Centre, Policy Brief, Issue 2, May 2013.

that Indo-Pacific region could be considered the future connectivity between the Indian Ocean and Pacific Ocean[4].

At present, there are a number of cooperation mechanisms such as ASEAN Regional Forum (ARF) with 27 member states, East Asia Summit (EAS) with 18 member states, which account for 55 percent of the world population and 55 percent of the world GDP. Cooperation among regional countries is also being promoted. However, in order to realise the concept of Indo-Pacific cooperation, all countries should work together to overcome difficulties and challenges.

Challenges to be Overcome

The first issue relates to territorial disputes on land and at sea in the region. At present, land border disputes still exist between some countries. There are also maritime territorial disputes in the East China Sea and East Sea (South China Sea). These are complicated issues bequeathed by history, and cannot be solved in a short period of time.

The second is the lack of trust among countries. Trust plays a decisive role in the cooperative relation among countries. The relations between countries will only be deepened and developed sustainably if there is mutual trust. There will not be real cooperation without trust and it will be difficult to resolve sensitive issues. For an ever growing Indo-Pacific cooperation, regional countries should promote the building of mutual trust and confidence. Publicity and transparency should be shown through various means such as formal or informal, state or non-state, and so on.

The third is to manage factors of impact. The two emerging major factors which potentially have impact on national and regional security and stability are the changes and the relationship with major powers. Over the past few years, the Indo-Pacific region has witnessed a number of changes, and economic and political reforms in many countries. In particular, competition for power between political camps may result in violence, social disorder, and even create security challenges for neighbouring countries. In the relation with major powers, medium and small countries have to take either

---

4 David Scott, Australia's embrace of the 'Indo-Pacific': new term, new region, new strategy? International Relations of the Asia-Pacific, Oxford Journals, 26 June 2013.

side or the other. In fact, bilateral relations between major powers, for example, US-China relations, play the role of shaping regional security mechanisms.

India's Role in Indo-Pacific Region

With a total area of 3,287,263 square kilometers (the seventh-largest country in the world) and a population of appropriately 1.2 billion (as of July 2013)[5], India is considered a regional power. India is ranked as number four in the top 10 largest economies in the world by nominal GDP (US $1,825 billion)[6]. Given its large area, robust economic growth, and willingness to take a greater role in international arena, India is destined to become a huge entity in the Indo-Pacific region. At the India-ASEAN Summit held in New Delhi in December 2012, Prime Minister Dr Manmohan Singh used the term "Indo-Pacific", an extension of the concept of Asia-Pacific region, and emphasised the importance of this region to India's stability and development[7].

As an economic engine, India has a great influence in the region. India has the largest population of working age (aged 15-54 is 58 percent). It is a major advantage of India, and the human resource which could enable India to become an information technology centre. India can make positive contributions to regional growth through increasing networks of Free Trade Agreements (FTAs) and Preferential Trade Agreements (PTAs) with ASEAN member countries and other countries, as well as through the increasing two way investment flow between India and ASEAN member states.

As far as strategic dimension is concerned, India occupies a unique geopolitical position stretching from the East coast of Africa to the West coast of Australia. As a founder and leader of the Non-Aligned Movement (NAM), India has high prestige and major role in the developing world. India and its relationships with other major powers have long been part of regional security mechanisms. More importantly, India is demonstrating its ability to be one of the

---

5 CIA World Factbook 2013: India

6 GDP based on Official Exchange Rate, India's GDP in 2012 is US$ 4,006 based on Purchasing Power Parity

7 Manmohan Singh, Opening statement at Plenary Session of India-ASEAN Commemorative Summit, 20 December 2012, The Government of India, New Delhi

influential leading powers in the world.

Over the past few years, under the thrust of its "Look East Policy", India has been playing an increasingly important role in the region through enhancing economic cooperation and security initiatives. India's presence in the region has become more obvious in many fields: politics, economics, commerce, defence, energy, and so on. Through its 'Look East Policy', India has gradually integrated into regional political structure in South East Asia, become ASEAN's formal dialogue partner in 1996 and an ARF member, and participated in debates on security situation in the region.

India institutionalised these links in the ASEAN+3 (China, Japan and South Korea) Summit in 2002. India is also a founder of EAS, first held in 2005, and has participated in the ASEAN Defence Ministers' Meeting Plus (ADMM+) since 2010 to exchange views on defence and security issues with ASEAN and other dialogue partners. After two decades of realising its "Look East Policy", India has gradually carried out regional economic integration, while at strategic level its increasing commitments in East Asia have laid out challenges which need to be addressed by India, especially those relate to India's stance toward US and China.

Promoting India-ASEAN Cooperation

The Association of Southeast Asian Nations (ASEAN) has emerged as an effective mode of cooperation, drawing the attention of the world in general and India in particular, since 1990s. In India's "Look East Policy", ASEAN is regarded to be a focal point. India-ASEAN cooperation is a dynamic relationship mostly aimed at integration. Over the past few years, ASEAN member states have been willing to cooperate with India on bilateral, regional and international issues, providing India with a geostrategic context to reconstruct its political, economic, cultural and historical relations with ASEAN. Political relations between India and ASEAN have seen considerable development in recent years. India and ASEAN have established dialogue and cooperation mechanisms such as ASEAN-India Summit, ASEAN Post Ministerial Conference (PMC)+1, Mekong-Ganga Cooperation Meeting, Bay of Bengal Initiative for Multi-Sectoral Technical and Economic Cooperation (BIMSTEC), and so on.

In terms of economic activities, over the past 20 years, India-ASEAN trade turnover has increased by 10 times. India's economic growth and ASEAN's economic recovery have strengthened their economic and financial relations. Within four years (2002-2005), India-ASEAN bilateral trade turnover increased over 150 percent from US$ 9.7 billion in 2002 to US $ 23 billion in 2005. India-ASEAN bilateral trade turnover in 2012 totaled US $ 80 billion, compared to US $ 47 in 2008. ASEAN accounts for 10 percent of India's trade. Foreign Direct Investment (FDI) from ASEAN to India has made up over 10 percent of India's total FDI over the past 10 years. Conversely, with about US $ 2.6 billion (2010), India ranked sixth among ASEAN's biggest foreign direct investors, and was ASEAN's seventh largest trading partner. India-ASEAN trade targets US $ 100 billion by 2015 and double by 2022[8]. India and ASEAN also promote cooperation in culture, society, science, technology, education and so on. India and ASEAN commemorated 20 years of Partnership in 2012. For India, this anniversary also marked two decades of implementing "Look East Policy" and India's efforts to strengthen relationship with neighbouring countries in Southeast Asia. Although India-ASEAN relationship has developed in many aspects - in both width and depth - over the past 20 years, a number of potentialities for cooperation should be exploited and brought into play. India and ASEAN should work more closely with each other in inter-regional initiatives. The two sides should promote cooperation in sub-regional initiatives such as Mekong-Ganga Cooperation Initiative, Initiative for ASEAN Integration, the South Asian Association for Regional Cooperation (SAARC), and so on. India can support ASEAN effectively and practically through mechanisms such as Lower Mekong Initiative, a mechanism with the participation of Japan, US, and South Korea, ASEAN-India Connectivity, and so on.

India-ASEAN trade relations have been growing significantly, but not at par with the two sides' potential. Although India's economy has been grows by 7-8 percent annually, the share of India in ASEAN total trade turnover accounts for only one percent. Negotiations for a Free Trade Agreement (FTA) between India and ASEAN fail to meet our expectations. India's FDI policy fails to create favourable

---

8 Manmohan Singh, Opening statement at Plenary Session of India-ASEAN Commemorative Summit, 20 December 2012, The Government of India, New Delhi

conditions for attracting FDI inflows from ASEAN.

In order to further elevate India-ASEAN relationship, making contribution to the realization of the concept of Indo-Pacific cooperation, both India and ASEAN should devote more effort to overcome difficulties and challenges, implement ASEAN-India Plan of Action aimed at promoting multi-faceted cooperation, and deepen ASEAN-India relations, contributing to the building of a peaceful and prosperous Indo-Pacific region.

Session - IV

Fifth Paper

Prof (Ms) Ruhanas Harun

The Indo–Pacific Region: Consolidating the Gains, Minimising Loses

Introduction

The focus of this paper is how security issues shape relations between countries of the Indo-Pacific region and the efforts made to promote and consolidate regional peace and security. It will identify some of the major issues concerned and analyse their threats to the region. Despite the existence of many unresolved issues, the region remains one of the most peaceful in the world. This is partly due to the fact that countries recognised the fact that the gains they have achieved through cooperative relationship will be lost if peace and security are compromised. The miniature title of this paper therefore could also be read as "the Indo-Pacific Region: Consolidating Gains and Minimising Loses Through Cooperative Relationship".

The Evolution of a Complex Regional Order

Before discussing the evolution of the regional order itself, allow me to briefly explain the term Indo-Pacific. To me the term Indo-Pacific, as it refers to the geographical area of a region that extends from Asia to the Pacific is relatively new. We are familiar with the geographical scope known as Asia—further divided into sub regions of South Asia, Southeast Asia, Northeast Asia, Central Asia and West Asia. However, this too has been substituted by another term, the Asia Pacific Region (APR), as it is widely used until now. Its geographical scope includes South Asian countries, East Asia and the Pacific nations, of which the US is a part. But it also includes countries such as Russia, Canada, Australia and New Zealand. Thus it is really a big family of nations encompassing countries connected to Asia and the Pacific.

Now we have a new terminology to understand, the Indo-Pacific Region (IPR) which would incorporate more or less the same countries that make up the APR. Interestingly, it also created some grudges among Asians because of the 'demise' of their beloved 'Asia' in the expression of IPR. The term also aroused a curiosity about the word "Indo" which many understand in terms of cultural elements as opposed to the plain geographical scope of APR or Asia. One is not sure if there is a hidden agenda behind the "Indo-Pacific" or intent of cultural imperialism! Maybe it can also simplify the understanding of the geographical content: a region that begins with the Indian sub-continent, bordering the Indian Ocean and ends somewhere in the Pacific Ocean. Whatever it is, for the purpose of this paper, I shall use the terms APR and IPR interchangeably to denote the geographical region that begins with the Indian sub-continent towards the east until the Pacific.

The IPR is indeed a vast area extending from the Indian Ocean in the West to the Pacific Ocean in the East. One of the characteristics of the region is its diversity of cultures, religions, ethnic groups, languages and political systems. In the past, almost all of these countries were colonised by the Europeans, thus adding to the diversity. The end of World War II saw the beginning of independence for these countries and rise of political systems chosen by the leaders of the time. The period coincided with the Cold War, further deepening the differences, prompting these countries to choose between the two camps: the communist camp led by the USSR and the 'free world' led by the US. Throughout the Cold War, ideologies played a major role in shaping threat perceptions and behaviour of states with regards to security and politics. They led to conflicts in the region in the forms of internal insurgencies, proxy wars, open conflict and great power rivalry. The most divisive and tragic, as a result of these was the Vietnam War that began in 1946 and ended in 1975. Another significant feature of these conflicts was the role of major powers, either through direct military intervention or intervention by other means. Two regional orders were created, one competing with the other for supremacy and dominance. This was to last until the end of the Cold War in 1990, with the fall of the Soviet Union.

By the end of the decade, East Asia in particular has emerged as an economically dynamic region, politically more mature and more peaceful. With the crumbling of the ideological divide, the post- Cold War era is more conducive to greater cooperation between states in the region. The end of the Cold War provided more opportunities and options in their external relations and domestic policies. The process of accommodation and harmonisation of policies and interests became more flexible. Today, more than two decades into the new 'world order', despite some left over security issues from the past, the Asia-Pacific region has achieved peace and prosperity. A new regional order is said to have emerged, but along with it, the emergence of new forms of threat to security which nations in the region continue to deal with.

Same Actors, Different Stage?

Before going on to discuss my vision of a stable and peaceful IPR, I would like to share with you the problems and opportunities facing several important regional players in helping to promote a peaceful, stable and secure IPR. The demise of the Cold War put an end to superpower rivalry, yet, as a Korean scholar commented, "we soon realised that the dissolution of that rivalry also meant the emergence of loose ends in several parts of the world." Mending these loose ends would pre-occupy the attention of major powers in the region.

China emerged as a major player in the Asia-Pacific region, and indeed in the world. Its rise, albeit peaceful, has caused concern to the US and to some other countries. They cast doubt as to whether China, with the new economic power it has acquired, can be a "responsible" power. A former US National Security adviser wondered "if China entertains wider aspirations given its view of the Chinese state as the global centre". He also believed that its economic momentum is bound to give it both greater physical power and increasing ambitions. Another major player in the region is Russia. The dismantling of the USSR, reduced the territory under Moscow's control, but has allowed Russia to remain as major power. During the Soviet era, Moscow's preoccupation in matters of defence and security was towards Europe. After the end of the Cold War, Europe became stable and emerged united and became more independent to deal with Russia. European-

Russian relations evolved from mutual fear and distrust to a more amenable position, and security thinking evolved beyond threats directed towards one another. The dismantling of the USSR created a series of states on the periphery of Russia, and this Russia as well as China cannot ignore. Besides, a large part of Russian territory is in the East (Asia).

As an economic power, Japan has "the potential of first class political power, but so far this has not happened". In fact, Japan is known as an "economic giant, a political dwarf." This unflattering remark about the country can be attributed to Japan's inability to turn its economic success into political influence. Post war Japan has been constrained by the American presence and security dependence on the US. But some also attributed it to Japan's own self-restraint that makes the country reluctant to pursue a greater political role in world affairs, thus it seems to eschew any aspirations for regional dominance. Again, this may not be the consensus today, within and outside Japan.

Japan's neighbour, South Korea, has also emerged as a newly industrialised country in East Asia, dubbed as an 'Asian tiger'. It enjoys close relations with the three major powers of the APR, namely China, Japan and US. While maintaining close security relations with the US, South Korea has important economic relations with China and Japan.

Not much has been said about India's emergence on the scene or what its aspirations are. India is in the process of establishing itself as a major power. Many view India as having the potential to become a great power capable of playing a bigger role in international affairs. Some may also see it as China's rival, although it is perceived to be benign and without the 'assertiveness" attributed to China. India, arguably, the most powerful state in South Asia, has also been described as a "regional hegemon of sorts, a semi-secret nuclear power" which became one "in order to intimidate Pakistan and to balance China. "As a citizen of an IPR country, I think it is the interest of IPR to pit India against China, or to pour oil over fire in India-Pakistan relations. These three countries are neighbours, sharing common problems, but with well managed relations, they may also share common benefits. Most importantly, whether they like it or not, especially in the case of Pakistan and India, they will have to live next door to each other, preferably in peaceful co-existence.

India, more than China, Japan or Russia, enjoys high credibility in being a benign power for several reasons. It is not perceived as threatening to US security interests and a challenge to US economic dominance in Asia. It is also the world's largest democracy, thus having shared values with the West. Unlike Japan, India has not invaded other countries in wars. For many in ASEAN, India has often been looked at with a nostalgic past in the cultural, social and religious domains. Thus there exist deep-rooted historical and cultural connections between India and Southeast Asian countries. Furthermore, India is seen as playing, if not entrusted with a major role in safeguarding the Indian Ocean, the western gateway of the IPR. In sum, India's behaviour and aspirations (who knows?) have not displayed signs of 'aggressive belligerency 'as some have accused China of. So the prospect of India's rise is less worrying, to say the least.

In summary, it is true to say that the end of the Cold War ushered in a new regional security environment, but the stage is still dominated by the same actors and issues carried on from the previous era. The rivalry of the same kind, a global rivalry for dominance among major powers still exists. Nevertheless, there are positive developments since then which led to rethinking, and in some cases, revising of attitudes and policies which in the past hampered the emergence of a desirable regional security order.

Geostrategic Choices

The US today is the only truly global power and it is not likely to let go of this dominance as it strives to maintain this position while at the same time tries to curb others that may threaten its position. Its pre-eminence as a global power with global interests has given the world a new pattern of relationship among nations. The choices they make today reflect in many ways this new pattern of relationship that has emerged in the last two decades.

In today's era of globalisation, nations do make choices to

safeguard their national interests. This option may come in the form of smart partnerships, either bilaterally, or multilaterally. Former enemies have become friends, as in the case of US and Vietnam and today the two countries enjoy close economic, political, social and security relations. Vietnam and China, who in the past were uneasy friends, seem to settle into a relationship of mutual respect. India, formerly seen as closer to Russia, has now warmed up to the US. The countries of Southeast Asia have been able to maintain friendly relations with the rest of the world.

The United States, as the main player in the APR/ IPR has decided upon a strategy of re-engagement of its own in the region. In 2011, the Obama administration announced the pivot to Asia policy, or rebalancing strategy as it is more popularly known. This policy is born out of concern of being left out in Asia, but also of the confidence it has in its relationship with Europe, the most important region for US. Washington also wants to reassure its Asian allies and friends that it is committed to Asia; and that it is still the power that matters in the region. The rise of China is of course an added catalyst to this re-balancing policy. With the frustrations and uncertainties about its role and influence in the Middle East, the US cannot afford to alienate or lose Asia, a region politically more stable and more reliable as friend.

Issues, Challenges and Limitations

Despite the positive trend of cooperative relationship among many nations in the region, there are some issues of concern that have the potential to threaten regional peace and security. The existence of unresolved issues in the form of territorial disputes remain as thorns in the flesh in the relations between those nations involved. The Taiwan issue is one. Although there is peace, it is an unsettled peace. Another threat to regional peace and security is the South China Sea dispute, currently involving six countries of the region—China, Vietnam, Malaysia, Philippines, Brunei and Taiwan. Although there is no war or open conflict among claimants, occasional clashes occur between some of them, in particular between China and Philippines. Bad relations between the two will complicate matters for the US and ASEAN. Philippines, a close friend and a US ally, is keen to have US involvement as guarantee to its security, if this is threatened.

China has developed close relations with ASEAN countries; as such a quarrel between China and an ASEAN member country will put the association in a difficult position. Another issue is the dispute between China and Japan over the sovereignty of the Senkaku islands (Diaoyu in Chinese) which has led to serious disagreement between them. What deterred them from engaging in open conflict is the realisation that if that happens, it will be mutually damaging to both and may lead to extra-regional power intervention. The Kashmir issue, although has not provoked a more visible concern and response in East Asia, continues to be a major stumbling block towards the improvement of relations between India and Pakistan. The two countries do not seem to be willing to come to an understanding on how to resolve the issue.

The Korean problem, a legacy of the Cold War is full of uncertainties and has the potential to destabilise the region. North Korea is highly unpredictable and its possession of nuclear weapons makes the situation even more precarious. North Korea remains a close friend of China, although in recent years China has developed strong economic and social ties with South Korea. South Korea remains a country protected under the US-RoK alliance and is of strategic importance to the US. To what extent are the two major powers willing to be dragged into an open conflict between North and South Korea remains a speculation. Will China risk conflict with US to defend North Korea, in the same manner if the US would risk getting involved in confrontation with China in defending South Korea? Failure of the US to do so will bring into question the relevance of US-RoK security alliance. Any significant change in South Korea's status, either through unification or shift into China's sphere of influence will change US role in East Asia. It is assumed that the US is determined to protect RoK, and the main reason guiding the US in this is not economic, but strategic. The US wants to remain in RoK, to make it a shield for US interests and possibly for Japan as well. The uncertainty in the Korean Peninsula also posed a dilemma for China. Taking sides would jeopardise Chinese position and interests and would potentially, even if unwillingly drag China into confrontation with the US. Abandoning North Korea is a possibility, but it will be so with a heavy conscience for the Chinese.

The unpredictability of the Korean situation may also allow for some optimism. Both North and South Korea have engaged each other in the past to try to resolve their differences and problematic relationship. In 2011, they attempted to cultivate cooperative relationship through economic, military and social initiatives, humanitarian assistance and private sector contacts. But these initiatives and efforts of the softening of policy have not changed the status quo or reduced uncertainty. Several factors contributed to this. One is the highly unpredictable behaviour of North Korea, including its leadership. North Korea has taken both a hard line and a soft line in its response to the South's initiatives. An example of the softer line was the North's agreement to engage in at least some kind of dialogue with South Korea. In 2011, military officials of the two countries held talks on the "issue of Cheonan case and the Yeonpyeong Island shelling and diffusing military tension on the Korean Peninsula". But despite these initiatives, North Korea maintained its hard-line stance against the South. It refused to admit responsibility for the Cheonan and Yongpyeong incidents. It refused to negotiate with South Korea on the nuclear issue.

But is it possible to hope for some change under the current leadership of Kim Jung Un, that he might take a new line of policy towards the South that will promote towards cultivating good relations with the South? Even though re-unification of the Koreas at the moment seems a bit remote, it cannot be totally excluded. Who would have thought of the peaceful German unification in 1989? Or would Korean unification go the Vietnamese way, by force? If there is no urgency or necessity for re-unification, then the status quo in Korea is acceptable so long as the security impact of its division is manageable. Currently countries within its proximity and beyond would not want another Korean war because it would lead to a lost situation for all.

Japan is equally concerned about the problem in the Korean peninsula. Besides being in the geographical proximity, Japan's relations with the two Korean states have not been smooth. There are edges to be mended. Irritations in their relations include sensitive historical issues and of recent event such as the kidnapping of Japanese citizens by DPRK authorities and its nuclear threat to Japan. With regards to North Korean nuclear issue, Japan maintains close ties with

South Korea and the US. The importance of Japanese-South Korean bilateral collaboration was confirmed at the meeting of Japanese Prime Minister Yoshihiko Noda and President Lee Myung-bak of South Korea in their meetings in Seoul and Kyoto in 2011. They also recognised the importance of co-operation in the area of defence. In their meetings in 2011, the two countries' defence ministers agreed to exchange opinions on several matters such as the United Nations peacekeeping operations, search and rescue drills and on the importance of exchanging military information. However, because the RoK government has to be mindful of deep- rooted mistrust of Japan among certain sections of the South Korean public, it apparently plans to proceed cautiously and gradually in promoting defence cooperation with Japan (NIDS : 2012 :32).

The unpredictability of the situation in the Korean Peninsula, the tension created, the obstacles to better cooperation and response of those involved may seem alarming, especially with North Korea's erratic behaviour. But North Korea is not allowed to do as it pleases, its actions are also constrained by the watchful eyes of its more powerful neighbours and a global power, as well its own realisation that aggressive behaviour is not acceptable to countries of the region and will cause harm to North Korea itself. As such one can say that there is a built-in deterrence mechanism of sorts that will at least make aggressive nations think twice before deciding on a self-destruct or suicidal policy, unless one is completely mad.

China's Rise: An Issue and a Challenge to Regional Security?

There are a lot of interpretations and perceptions about what constitute threats to regional order and security, but also what will help to maintain the stability of the region. China's relationship with the US is seen as the most crucial element to maintain this stability. More often than not, the rise of China and its implications are explained from the perspective of the national interests of major powers such as the US and Europe. Smaller and less powerful countries, especially those in the region will have to adjust to the strategies of these countries the environment they created. Still, countries are entitled to their own interpretations and to act according to their own national interests.

China's rise and its implications dominated debates and

discussion. Despite the insistence of the Chinese that their rise is 'peaceful', the US and Europe feel concerned about China's potential challenge to their dominance politically and economically. Such concern has been projected to and influenced other countries in the region. In Europe, I have been frequently asked as to why we (in ASEAN, especially in Malaysia) do not seem to worry about China's rise and its potential danger. My escape from this difficult question has always been to borrow the idea of former Prime Minister of Malaysia, Dr Mahathir Mohammad in saying that we "see China as an opportunity, not a threat." The opportunity lies not only in the economic and trade relations with China, but also by maintaining friendly relations with China, ASEAN countries hope and expect the Asian power to remain benign.

Stability in Sino-US relations is critical to the emergence of a stable international environment. In September 2011, China released a white paper "China's Peaceful Development", in which it emphasised the importance of "establishing and developing a new type of relationship among the major countries." China focuses in particular, on its relations with the United States. According to China, this relationship is "the most important bilateral relationship, impacting not only relations between the two countries, but also on the peace and development of the entire world".

But differences between the US and China with regards to many issues remain. The most profound policy divergence is on the issue of Taiwan. China maintains that Taiwan is an integral part of China. But China also recognises the need to improve and stabilise its relations with the US. In 2010, China has resumed military exchanges which had been suspended since the US approved weapons sale to Taiwan earlier that year. But irritations in their relations remain, for example, the US military surveillance in China's periphery, new weapons sale to Taiwan, among other issues.

In addition to the concern about what it will do with its newly acquired status of an economic giant, China's military modernisation has also raised questions about its intent and purpose. China has reassured regional countries that its military modernisation is for defensive and not for offensive purposes. Whether military modernisation of China is a factor that threatens peace and security in APR/IPR is again open to interpretations. Suspicions towards China do exist among some countries of Southeast Asia prompted by the so-called "assertive actions" of China in the South China Sea. But this did not stop cooperation in other areas.

Thus, despite the many worries and irritations, both major and minor, China's rise has not led to any aggressive ventures on the part of Beijing. Suspicions remain and predictions about what China will do amidst these mixed blessings of being a powerful country will continue. How it will affect the IPR is also a matter of speculation, but one may take reassurance in China's repeated reminder that it has never aggressed or conquered another country.

Other Issues of Concern

Apart from the doom and gloom of traditional security issues that have pre-occupied major powers, new forms of security threat emerged to dominate security thinking of lesser powers in the region. The ASEAN region is familiar with these security threats which include terrorism, piracy smuggling, human trafficking, illegal immigrants and centre-periphery conflicts. History, geography, social and economic conditions are some of the major factors shaping and influencing the emergence and visibility of these threats.

After the 9/11 incident, terrorism and extremism in all forms are looked upon as the most serious threat to security of states. The US led the world in the Global War on Terror (GWOT), also in all its forms. For a while, this issue seemed to dominate all other issues of security and created a sense of urgency of the threat and in dealing with it, sometimes regardless of the specific conditions of different countries involved. Post 9/11, the issue of extremism and acts of terrorism are largely associated with the rise of Islamic extremism. Regional countries with large Muslim populations such as Indonesia, Malaysia, Pakistan, and India have had to deal with this. Other countries with Muslim minorities such as China, Thailand, Philippines and Singapore too have been keeping a close watch. Even countries such as Japan, Korea, Laos and Vietnam, whose Muslim population is negligible, joined in the fray. Regional countries established cooperation to combat the threat of terrorism through intelligence exchange, financial support and awareness programs on the issue. Malaysia for example established in 2005 the Southeast Asian Regional Centre for Counter Terrorism (SEARCCT) under the Ministry of Foreign Affairs of Malaysia. This endeavour was supported by the US. Its activities consisted among others, awareness campaign about the scourge of terrorism and extremism. However, after more than a decade of this global war on terror, the attention towards the issue seems to be waning, though states are still vigilant about its potential threat. A recent initiative by the Malaysian government to create GMM is aimed to create such awareness and to rally nations to fight against extremism confirms this.

The concept note of this conference also mentioned that "terrorist groups have established deep roots in the IPR and are operating across national boundaries with increasing impunity." Here I would like to share some experience from ASEAN region. It may be true that in the Indian sub-continent, especially in Pakistan and Afghanistan, and in some parts of India, extremism and religious militancy do have deep roots. This is not the case in the ASEAN region. Diversity and tolerance have long been an accepted fact of life in many ASEAN countries. Indonesia, the largest Muslim country in the world is also known for its diversity, tolerance and home to a trend known as "liberal Islam". Religious extremism and militancy are not inherent to Indonesian society, as well as in many other Southeast Asian countries. External influences brought such trend into Indonesia and in the process lit up the fire, resulting in acts of terrorism such as the Bali and the JW Marriot Hotel bombings in Jakarta. The perpetrators have been dealt with and terrorist organisations in Indonesia have come under close watch and control of the state. Perhaps things are different in Pakistan or Afghanistan, which do not share the same political system and the socio-cultural and economic conditions of Indonesia and Malaysia. The fact that terrorism in these two important Muslim countries of ASEAN is not deep rooted, coupled with the will of the state and society to rid them of this menace contributed to the effectiveness of dealing with it.

As for the painful memories, (also alluded to in the concept paper), they can be reduced, if not, erased if states take the initiative not to use them for political gains. The new younger generation is receptive to forward looking ideas and programs, even in situations where they are conditioned by states to think or behave in a certain manner. Exposure to youth on international issues that have impact on their surroundings can generate understanding and tolerance among communities and nations. It takes a long time to produce the desired results, but it must begin somewhere. At this juncture, I would like to cite the examples of Thailand, Malaysia and Singapore in their effort of building bridges among their peoples, thus creating a sense of hope and confidence in each other, despite the issues that caused strains in the relations between these countries.

Massive military build-up has been cited as an international security concern. IPR consist of big countries, some suspected of having "assertive behaviour coupled with willingness to use force. Fortunately, so far the assertive behaviour and aggressive intention remain as perceptions. The dividends of many years of peace and prosperity enjoyed by IPR has to a certain extent seeped into the thinking of states and peoples to regard peace as fundamental to their own survival.

Building and Preserving a Stable Regional Environment

The IPR has already put in place institutions which could be the basis of building regional peace, stability and security. The task now is to make use of these available mechanisms, the existence of cordial bilateral relations and the awareness of the inter -linkages and interdependency created in so many domains. The IPR should strive to strengthen regionalism and trust building, go for moderation, improve governance, devise a code of conduct and ensure that it is scrupulously observed by all, and importantly, avoid unflattering remarks, veiled or open, towards one another.

The challenge currently facing the Asia-Pacific is the question of how to manage the new situation with a view to preserve the stable environment in order to ensure the continued prosperity and mutual security. In response to this, countries in the region seek assurances of their security in various ways. Many are taking advantage of their increasing wealth to modernise their defence capabilities. While it is not possible to stop countries from increasing their defence capabilities especially when they are economically powerful as well, there is a need for dialogue and co-operation to prevent instability. In this regard, the formation of ARF in 1994 could well serve the purpose. At the same time, various confidence building measures are being explored to strengthen the foundations for regional peace and security. Apart from multilateral engagement, the enhancement of bilateral relations among regional states would contribute to this quest for peace and security.

Two decades after the end of the Cold War and the ushering in of the 'new world order', the regional security order is still evolving, taking into consideration the emergence of new actors and their visions of the kind of regional or world order that would commensurate with their position and influence. But as the world becomes more interlinked, there is a realisation among nations that they cannot hurt others without hurting themselves in the process. This in itself is a strong dampening impact upon aggressive behaviour. Even without the existence of a 'formal code of conduct', countries in the region are aware of the impact and the importance of inter-connectedness and interdependence in ensuring their survival and the continued prosperity of the region. This is an improved evolution in the attitude and mental framework for the region as compared to the early years of the post Cold War era. It was not uncommon in those days to advocate for a system that will be put in place "must be able to temper the arrogance and the assertive belligerence that can sometime typify the demeanour of those who have just scaled new heights of power".

Regionalism as an Option

The question now is how peace and security can be maintained in this region? Regionalism and regional integration are two possibilities that have been tried and with considerable success in promoting peace, security and prosperity. After World War II, the region has known several regional organisations aimed to harness the cooperative relations among members. In the nineties, the ASEAN was the toast of the town in so far as what a successful regional organisation can be. ASEAN has since its establishment in 1967 expanded from the five founding members (Indonesia, Malaysia, Thailand, Philippines, and Singapore) to what is now ASEAN 10. Despite some criticism of its being "too flexible" to be effective, it has been successful in uniting countries of diverse communities and political systems under one vision. More importantly, its diplomacy of "ASEAN Way" has helped built a sense of belonging among members. In addition, ASEAN plays an important role in regional initiatives, especially in security domain. It is looking forward towards the realisation of the ASEAN Community by 2015. SCO, established in 2001, is another example of regionalism that can help promote cooperation and discuss issues of common interests and concerns. There are a number of other sub-regional organisations with the same expressed aim and purpose, although they seem to be slightly 'laid-back' due to disagreement among import.

Alliances, especially formal military ones are no longer fashionable or desirable in this day and age. Forming such alliances would raise suspicion as alliance traditionally is designed to ally against someone. The presence of such alliances in some regions of the IPR has increasingly come under scrutiny as to the suitability and relevance in current regional security situation. The RoK-US alliance and US-Japan security treaty are two of these Cold War legacies which are still in operation. Malaysia, Singapore, Australia, New Zealand and the United Kingdom are still members of the Five Power Defence Arrangement (FPDA) established in 1971 in view of the then existing security situation. Today, the FPDA still exists, but its activities have been adjusted to suit the new political and security environment of today. They still conduct benign activities such as joint exercise, visits etc., activities which are not unfamiliar in the IPR. The US, French and Chinese navy ships do frequent the waters of Indian Ocean, Straits of Malacca, South China Sea and the Pacific on friendly visits. Such visits are important and should be continued because they make us aware of the potential danger, but at the same time they tell us that everyone wants peace and goodwill.

The Asia-Pacific multilateral institutions centred upon the principles of consensus, consultation and dialogue, as contained in the diplomacy of 'ASEAN way'. This refers to an approach to dispute settlement and regional co-operation developed by the members of ASEAN with view to ensuring regional peace and stability. The 'ASEAN way' consists of a code of conduct for inter-state behaviour as well as a decision-making process based on consultation and consensus. Principles include non-interference in the domestic affairs of each other, non-use of force, peaceful settlement of disputes, and respect for sovereignty and territorial integrity of member states. These are not new, as they can also be found in the United Charter and in other political and security regional organisations. But there is no harm in reminding. By harnessing commonalities and minimising differences, ASEAN has brought together countries of different political systems and diverse communities to work together towards a common destiny as envisaged in the ASEAN Community. But it has also extended cooperation with other countries through initiatives such as ASEAN Plus, ASEM, ADMM Plus etc. to share and further consolidate peace and stability in the region. IPR is not lacking in regional or multilateral organisations to channel any desire to work together, therefore should take advantage of their existence for dialogues and consultations, and to coordinate actions whenever possible. It can be a platform for 'trust building', a slow process, but one that is not impossible to achieve.

Looking at the political, economic and security evolution of the IPR, I think changes have been for the better. Countries formally foes become friends, and those who remain foes do not cherish such an idea and are not comfortable with the situation. The existence of multi polarity in the IPR means that relations tend to move towards that of equal rather than subordination. The increasing interdependence among nations in the region would moderate aggressive behaviour of those who might want to dominate others. The process of democratisation, has which has taken place in many countries, has contributed to better governance and transparency. The peace and stability, economic progress in many countries of the IPR has created more confidence among states to be more open, thus providing greater opportunity for interactions among peoples. This is indeed an important foundation for long lasting cooperative relations among nations and peoples. The way for a peaceful, co-operative and prosperous IPR has already been paved; it is up to the nations of the region to consolidate to consolidate the gains so far achieved.

Session - IV

Discussion

Issue Raised

What is the nature of the security architecture in the West Pacific?

Response

We have institutions like ARF and ASEAN there. The very existence of ASEAN is based on non-interference. The regional security architecture follows the principle of peaceful resolution of disputes and code of conduct to be followed by the member states. We have forums like 'ASEAN+' because we want to spread goodwill. We do not reject anybody and are all embracing in approach.

Issue Raised

Don't you think that Indian Navy's strength is small and we need to do more to instill confidence in South Asian countries?

Response

Our Navy has grown in time and has acquired important capabilities. It is important to have maritime security architecture so that resources of all the stakeholder countries are pooled in for a common cause. This creates interdependence and ensures security.

Issue Raised

North Korea's nuclear status is going to stay and will not change. Is South Korea thinking about developing nuclear weapons in future?

Response

If North Korea wants to discuss non proliferation, South Korea will support it. The problem is confidence. North Korea does not want to dismantle its nuclear weapons. There may be little possibility of North Korea coming to the table for talks. India is an important candidate in helping North Korea to come to the discussion table.

Issue Raised

What is Indian role in the ASEAN?

Response

India is an emerging power but not much is known about its aspirations about ASEAN. There is no negative opinion about India's rise and it is an opportunity for ASEAN.

Issue Raised

How can nuclearisation be stopped in the Indo Pacific region?

Response

We should do everything to stop nuclearisation anywhere in the world. But, that should not be done by containment and isolation but by engagement. Let us start with the things that are common and then come on to these issues.

Session - IV

Chairman's Concluding Remarks

Ambassador Leela K Ponappa, IFS (Retd)

No power has risen peacefully and history has proven that. In today's world due to communication and proximity, there are influences that can be brought upon the members of the global community to behave in a proper way, namely unilateral alteration of status quo through violent means. Certain initiatives have been taken with China's engagement with the ASEAN. There were some thoughts about nuclearisation and denuclearisation as well. I would recall India's persistent position on the subject, namely, disband all the nuclear weapons. The Non Proliferation Treaty (NPT) from the start has had a very flawed foundation. In today's world, you cannot have discriminatory regime of nuclear apartheid. Solutions are there but I think it is a question whether the political will exists to achieve them.

We have heard mention of inclusiveness in most of the papers. The whole ASEAN movement started with the South East Asian states getting together and forming the ASEAN. Whether we call it Indo-Pacific or Asia Pacific and what type of security architecture these countries will decide on is all work in progress.

USI should be congratulated for putting together this panel that allows for raising these issues in a collaborative manner. Obviously, there is not going to be agreement across the board but I do believe that the intent of institutions like the USI is to try and determine equilibrium. I thank the panel for their substantive contribution and you all for being a good audience.

VALEDICTORY SESSION

Vote of Thanks   Lieutenant General PK Singh, PVSM, AVSM (Retd), Director, USI.

Vote of Thanks

Lieutenant General PK Singh, PVSM, AVSM (Retd)
Director, USI

Ladies and gentleman, I will not keep you waiting longer than a minute. I must firstly thank the panelists and guests who have come from outside India. I also thank each one of you who sat through the session. This shows the quality of our panelists and papers they have presented. Please join me in showing appreciation for our friends who have come from abroad. I thank you for being here and I wish you all the very best. Please join us for a cup of belated high tea and thank you once again.